Banning Foreign Pharmacies from Sponsored Search: The Online Consumer Response*

Abstract

Increased competition from the Internet has raised a concern of product quality for online prescription drugs. The Food and Drug Administration (FDA) prohibits the importation of unapproved drugs into the US and the National Association of Boards of Pharmacy (NABP) emphasizes their illegality and cites examples of unsafe drugs from rogue pharmacies. An investigation by the Department of Justice (DOJ) revealed that Google was allowing unapproved Canadian pharmacies to advertise on their search engine and target US consumers. Because of heightened concern to protect consumers, Google agreed to ban non-NABP-certified pharmacies from their sponsored search listings in February 2010 and settled with the DOJ in August 2011. We study how the ban on non-NABP-certified pharmacies from sponsored search listings affects consumer search on the Internet.

Using click-through data from comScore, we find that non-NABP-certified pharmacies receive fewer clicks after the ban, and this effect is heterogeneous. In particular, pharmacies not certified by the NABP, but certified by other sources (other-certified sites), experience a reduction in total clicks, and some of their lost paid clicks are replaced by organic clicks. These effects do not change significantly after the DOJ settlement. In contrast, pharmacies not certified by any of the four major certification agencies suffer a greater reduction in both paid and organic clicks, and the reduction was exacerbated after the DOJ settlement. These results suggest that the ban has increased the search cost for other-certified sites, but at least some consumers overcome the search cost by switching from paid to organic links. In addition to search cost, the ban may have increased concerns for uncertified sites and discouraged consumers from reaching them via both paid and organic links.

JEL: D83, I18, K32, L81

Keywords: Online Prescription Drug, Internet Search, Foreign Pharmacy, Drug Safety

---

*We are grateful to Daniel Hosken, Jason Chan, Ben Handel, Matthew Gentzkow, William Vogt, and attendants at the 2013 White Conference, the 2013 Southern Economics Association Annual Conference and the 2014 American Economic Association Conference for constructive comments. All errors are ours.

†Chesnes: Federal Trade Commission, 600 Pennsylvania Avenue, N.W., Washington, DC 20580, mchesnes@ftc.gov. Dai and Jin: Department of Economics, University of Maryland, College Park, MD 20742, dai@econ.umd.edu, jin@econ.umd.edu. The opinions expressed here are those of the authors and not necessarily those of the Federal Trade Commission or any of its Commissioners.

1 Introduction

The Internet has led to a dramatic increase in the number of retailers available to consumers in many industries. The proliferation of competition may benefit consumers in several ways including lower prices. However, there is also the concern that the quality of the new product offerings may be lower, though difficult to discern by consumers. The concern is particularly acute for online prescription drugs, a market where poor product quality may lead to adverse health outcomes.

The high price of brand name prescription drugs has motivated US consumers to search for cheaper supplies from foreign pharmacies, despite the fact that personal importation is illegal. The Federal Food, Drug, and Cosmetic Act (FD&C Act) prohibits the importation of unapproved drugs into the US.[1] In particular, section 355(a) states: "No person shall introduce or deliver for introduction into interstate commerce any new drug, unless an approval of an application ... is effective with respect to such drug."[2] The FDA further states that interstate shipment includes importation and the FD&C Act applies to "any drugs, including foreign-made versions of U.S. approved drugs, that have not received FDA approval to demonstrate they meet the federal requirements for safety and effectiveness."[3]

Based on data from IMS Health, Skinner (2006) estimated that sales to US consumers from 278 confirmed or suspected Canadian-based Internet pharmacies reached CDN$507 million in the 12 month periods ending June 2005.[4] More than half of the sales were on top-selling brand-name prescription drugs consumed primarily by seniors. According to Skinner (2005), Canadian prices for the 100 top-selling brand-name drugs were on average 43% below US prices for the same drugs. Consistently, Quon et al. (2005) compared 12 Canadian Internet pharmacies with 3 major online US drug chain pharmacies and found that Americans can save an average of approximately 24% per unit of drug if they purchase the 44 most-commonly purchased brand-name medications from Canada. The large price difference between US and Canada has motivated not only individual Americans to order brand name prescription drugs from foreign pharmacies but also a large number of bills introduced by state or federal legislators in favor of legalizing or facilitating the cross-border drug trade with Canada.[5] Recent articles in the press also argue against the ban on unapproved foreign drugs, but the FDA maintains that drugs sold via unapproved pharmacies are often not equivalent to those sold legally in the US.[6]

While drug sales from foreign pharmacies have been growing, the National Association of Boards

---

[1] See http://www.fda.gov/RegulatoryInformation/Legislation/FederalFoodDrugandCosmeticActFDCAct.

[2] See http://www.gpo.gov/fdsys/pkg/USCODE-2010-title21/pdf/USCODE-2010-title21-chap9-subchapV-partA-sec355.pdf.

[3] See http://www.fda.gov/ForIndustry/ImportProgram/ucm173743.htm.

[4] This number was measured in standardized manufacturer-level prices and did not include "foot traffic" sales to US consumers through regular "brick-and-mortar" border pharmacies in Canada. Sales measured by final retail prices to US customers was not available but is certainly higher than CDN$507.

[5] According to Skinner (2006), the number of state and federal bills on this topic increased from 3 in 2002 to 84 in 2005.

[6] See a New York Times Opinion article: http://www.nytimes.com/2014/03/25/opinion/scare-tactics-over-foreign-drugs.html and the FDA's response: http://www.nytimes.com/2014/04/03/opinion/unsafe-foreign-drugs.html.

of Pharmacy (NABP) emphasizes the illegality of buying foreign drugs and highlights the danger of rogue pharmacies. In particular, NABP (2011) reviewed 7,430 Internet pharmacies as of December 2010 and found 96.02% of them operating out of compliance with US state and federal laws and/or NABP patient safety and pharmacy practice standards. Among these non-NABP-recommended pharmacies, 2,429 (34%) had server locations in a foreign country, 1,944 (27%) had a physical address out of US, 4,005 (56%) did not provide any physical address, 5,982 (84%) did not require a valid prescription, 4,397 (62%) issued prescriptions via online consultation, 3,210 (50%) offered foreign or non-FDA-approved drugs, 5,928 (83%) did not offer medical consultation, and 1,129 (16%) did not have secure sites. Independent research, mostly from medical researchers rather than economists, confirmed some of the NABP concerns, although the data gathered for these studies were often of a much smaller sample size. In particular, Orizio et al. (2011) reviewed 193 articles about Internet pharmacies, of which 76 were based on original data. The articles with original data suggested that geographic characteristics were concealed in many websites, at least some websites sold drugs without a prescription and an online questionnaire was a frequent tool used to replace a prescription. On drug quality, researchers often found inappropriate packaging and labeling, however, the chemical composition was found to differ from what is ordered in only a minority of studied samples.

Internet search engines, such as Google, are one avenue consumers use to reach Internet pharmacies. Upon submitting a query, a user is presented with two types of results. The first are organic results whose ranks are solely a function of search engine's relevance algorithm. The second type are called paid or sponsored links, which appear based on both the relevance of the link to the query and a monetary bid placed by the owner of the link. If the user clicks on a sponsored link, the link owner pays the search engine their bid. An example of a Google search results page is shown in Figure 1.

An investigation by the DOJ revealed that, as early as 2003, Google was allowing unapproved Canadian pharmacies to advertise on their search engine and target US consumers. While Canadian pharmacies face regulations within Canada, importation of drugs into the US is illegal because the FDA cannot ensure their safety and effectiveness. In addition, some pharmacies that claimed to be based in Canada were actually selling drugs from other foreign countries that may have lacked sufficient regulation. Because of heightened concern to protect consumers, Google agreed to ban non-NABP-certified pharmacies from their sponsored search listings in February 2010. Eighteen months later (August 24, 2011), Google settled with the DOJ by "forfeiting $500 million generated by online ads & prescription sales by Canadian online pharmacies."[7]

At first glance, the ban is a form of a minimum quality standard. Both Leland (1979) and Shapiro (1986) showed that a minimum quality standard (and its variant forms such as occupational licensing) can eliminate poor quality products, encourage high quality sellers to enter the market, and expand consumer demand because consumers anticipate higher quality under the regulation. These effects tend to benefit consumers who appreciate high quality. However, a minimum quality standard

---

[7]http://www.justice.gov/opa/pr/2011/August/11-dag-1078.html, retrieved December 28, 2013.

can also increase barriers to entry and reduce competition (Stigler 1971, Peltzman 1976). Even if the standard improves average quality on the market, it raises the market price and potentially hurts price-sensitive consumers by denying them access to low quality products. If the minimum quality standard is set by the industry, the harm can be even greater as the industry has incentives to set too high a standard in order to reduce competition (Leland 1979).

A number of empirical studies have attempted to test the theory of minimum quality standards by examining price, quantity, quality, and market structure, but all of them assumed that the standard is well enforced in reality.[8] This assumption does not hold for online pharmacies: after the ban, consumers can still access non-NABP-certified pharmacies through organic search. Moreover, the ban affected only one channel through which consumers can gather safety information about online pharmacies. Other channels of information includes consumer experience, word of mouth, and alternative certification agencies. Specifically, Google used a private certification agency – PharmacyChecker.com – to filter rogue pharmacies before the ban. This abandoned practice is more lenient than the ban because PharmacyChecker certifies both US and foreign pharmacies while NABP automatically disqualifies any foreign pharmacies.[9] Even after the ban, Google uses the Canadian Internet Pharmacy Association (CIPA) to screen sponsored ads that target Canadian consumers, but the CIPA-certified pharmacies are not NABP-certified for US customers because they are foreign.

According to Leland (1979) and Shapiro (1986), one welfare loss from a minimum quality standard is the denial of low quality products to price-sensitive consumers. With organic links and alternative information channels, this denial is likely incomplete for online pharmacies, which offers us an excellent opportunity to study how pharmacies compliant with the minimum quality standard (NABP-certified pharmacies) coexist or even compete with non-NABP-certified pharmacies.

How easy is it to switch to organic links when sponsored links of the same website are no longer available? A rising literature has shown that sponsored links accounted for 15% of all clicks (Jansen and Sprink 2009), consumers had a preference against sponsored links (Jansen and Resnick 2006), consumers appreciated sponsored links as advertisements if they were relevant (Jansen, Brown and Resnick 2007), and organic and sponsored links from the same website of a national retailer were complements in consumer clicks (Yang and Ghose 2010). Two studies released by Google painted a

---

[8] Law and Kim (2005) explored the effects of occupational licensing in the Progressive Era and showed that the licensing regulation had improved markets when consumers faced increasing difficulty in judging the quality of professional services. Law and Marks (2009) examined the introduction of state-level licensing regulation during the late nineteenth and mid-twentieth centuries and found that licensing laws often helped female and black workers, particularly in occupations where worker quality was hard to ascertain. On the negative side, Pashigian (1979) reported that state-specific occupational licensing had a quantitatively large effect in reducing the interstate mobility of professionals; Shepard (1978) estimated that the price of dental services and mean dentist income were between 12 and 15 percent higher in non-reciprocity jurisdictions when other factors are accounted for; Adams et al. (2003) compared state-by-state regulation on midwifery licensing and found that more stringent licensing regulation led to fewer births by midwifery, which led them to conclude that licensing regulation had a detrimental effect by restricting entry and competition.

[9] In this sense, Google adoption of the NABP standard is similar to a switch from certification to a minimum quality standard, on which Shapiro (1986) argued that certification can be more welfare-improving because it allows the whole spectrum of quality to be known and available to consumers.

somewhat different picture. Chan, et al. (2012) found that 81% of sponsored impressions and 66% of sponsored clicks occurred in the absence of an associated organic link on the first page of search results. This suggests that most sponsored links are from websites that are not easy to find in organic search. Chan, et al. (2011) examined 446 incidences between October 2010 to March 2011 where advertisers temporarily paused their sponsored ads to determine their effectiveness. From these incidences, they found that 89% of the traffic generated by sponsored ads was not replaced by organic clicks (leading to the same destination website) when the ads were paused. This suggests that organic and sponsored traffic are not necessarily substitutes. If many non-NABP-certified pharmacies do not appear in high ranked organic results, the ban of their appearance in sponsored listings could be an effective tool to minimize consumer clicks on them in organic search.

It is worth noting that the organic-sponsored substitution is not necessarily the only margin for the ban to take effect. The ban could have other market-wide effects depending on how consumers digest the information conveyed by the ban. One message conveyed to consumers by the ban may be that NABP-certified pharmacies are believed to be safer than non-NABP-certified pharmacies, and this message should be more salient after the Google-DOJ settlement. However, the ban may also send an indirect message about the overall danger of the online prescription drug market, or inform consumers that some alternative and potentially cheaper pharmacies exist although they are not allowed to advertise in sponsored search. Moreover, the ban groups all other-certified pharmacies with uncertified pharmacies, potentially making it more difficult for consumers to differentiate quality among the non-NABP-certified websites. These economic forces, as well as the technical difficulty of substituting sponsored clicks for organic clicks, may affect consumer search in different directions. This leaves the net effect and the source of the net effect an empirical question.

Overall, the goal of this paper is to examine how consumer search on the Internet changes after the ban of non-NABP-certified pharmacies from sponsored advertising. In particular, we classify pharmacy sites into three tiers: NABP-certified (tier-A), other-certified (tier-B), and uncertified (tier-C). NABP-certified sites refer to US pharmacies that receive approval from NABP or the NABP-endorsed certifier, LegitScript.[10] NABP-certified sites are free to advertise in sponsored search listings before and after the ban. Other-certified sites refer to foreign or domestic pharmacies that are certified by PharmacyChecker.com or CIPA, but not by NABP or LegitScript. All the rest are classified as uncertified sites. Although both other-certified and uncertified sites are banned from Google's sponsored search after February 2010, we distinguish them for two reasons: first, uncertified sites were prohibited from sponsored listings even before the ban, but the screening was imperfect. In comparison, other-certified websites were allowed to bid for sponsored ads until the ban. Second, other-certified sites may be subject to a higher safety standard in the eyes of consumers that purchase drugs online and therefore the ban could have different effects on them as compared to the other two types of pharmacy sites.

Using 2008-2012 comScore data, we find that the banned pharmacies experience a reduction in

---

[10] As detailed in Section 2, NABP endorses LegitScript to act on its behalf in screening websites for search engines, so we treat approval from LegitScript the same as certification from NABP.

the number of total clicks after the ban but the effect is heterogeneous. In particular, tier-B sites experience a smaller reduction in total clicks with some of the lost paid click-throughs replaced by organic clicks. These effects do not change significantly after the Google-DOJ settlement. In contrast, tier-C sites receive fewer traffic in both paid and organic clicks, and the reduction is even greater after the DOJ settlement.[11] We also explore whether the effect of the ban depends on what drug names consumers search for on the Internet. Drug queries that led to more clicks on non-NABP-certified pharmacies before the ban are most affected by the ban, but chronic drug queries are less affected by the ban than non-chronic drugs. Overall, we conclude that the ban has increased search cost for tier-B sites but at least some consumers overcome the search cost by switching from paid to organic links. In addition to search cost, the ban may have increased health or safety concerns for tier-C sites, which may explain why consumers are discouraged from clicking those links.

The paper proceeds as follows. In section 2, we provide background on the online market for prescription drugs as well as changes to Google's policy regarding sponsored search ads from online pharmacies. We lay out our econometric framework in section 3 including a model we use to separate the effects of the ban on consumer beliefs and search costs. Section 4 describes the data provided by comScore and results are presented in section 5. Section 6 concludes.

2 Background

2.1 The Online Market of Prescription Drugs

According to IMS, prescription drug sales in the US has grown from $135 billion in 2001 to $307 billion in 2010 (IMS 2011). A literature review by Orizio et al. (2011) found that the percent of general population using online pharmacies was often reported to be between 4% and 6%. Although the percentage is small, the total volume of sales can be huge. According to Skinner (2006), sales to US consumers from 278 Canadian or seemingly-Canadian pharmacies reached CDN$507 million in the 12 month periods ending June 2005. The US$500 million fine that Google agreed to pay in 2011 also indicates the size of the online prescription drug market, as the fine is calculated by the revenue received by Google for selling sponsored ads to Canadian pharmacies and the estimated revenue that Canadian pharmacies got from their sales to US consumers.[12]

One major concern of online purchase is drug safety. As described in NABP (2011) and Orizio et al. (2011), drug safety can be potentially compromised by a relaxed prescription requirement, insufficient medical consultation, incorrect packaging and labeling, wrong ingredients, or no delivery at all. Some rogue websites also aim to steal consumer credit card information for identity theft. Although the FD&C Act prohibits the importation of unapproved drugs, when determining the legality of personal shipments, "FDA personnel may use their discretion to allow entry of shipments

---

[11] Paid clicks on tier-C sites should be zero immediately following the ban, though a small number of paid clicks are still observed.

[12] CNN report August 24, 2011, accessed at http://money.cnn.com/2011/08/24/technology/google_settlement/index.htm.

of violative FDA regulated products when the quantity and purpose are clearly for personal use, and the product does not present an unreasonable risk to the user."[13] Therefore, a consumer who purchases a drug from a foreign pharmacy for personal use faces some uncertainty regarding the likely reaction by the FDA.

To address safety concerns, the FDA also publicizes anecdotes of unsafe pharmaceuticals on the Internet and warns consumers against rogue websites (which could be foreign or domestic). They also advise consumers to avoid any foreign websites and only make online purchases from the US websites certified by the NABP. The NABP certification ensures that a US website comply with laws in both the state of their business operation and the states to that they ship medications. As of February 29, 2012, NABP has certified 30 online pharmacies, 12 of which are run by large PBM companies (open to members only) and the rest include national chain pharmacies (such as cvs.com and walgreens.com) and large online-only pharmacies (such as drugstore.com).

Another private certification agency, LegitScript.com[14], is similar to the NABP in terms of only approving US-based websites and endorsed by the NABP to screen pharmacy websites after the Google ban. As of March 5, 2012, the home page of LegitScript announced that they monitored 228,419 Internet pharmacies among which 40,233 were active. Within active websites, LegitScript found 221 legitimate (0.5%), 1,082 potentially legitimate (2.7%) and 38,929 not legitimate (96.8%). Their certification criterion includes a valid license with local US jurisdictions, valid registration with the US Drug Enforcement Administration (DEA) if dispensing controlled substances, valid contract information, valid domain name registration, requiring a valid prescription, only dispensing FDA approved drugs, and protecting user privacy according to the HIPAA Privacy Rule (45 CRF 164). There are more LegitScript-certified websites than NABP-certified websites, probably because the NABP requires interested websites to apply and pay verification fees while LegitScript's approval is free and does not require website application. Because the NABP praises the work of LegitScript and endorses the use of LegitScript by domain name registrars to assist in identifying illegally operating websites, throughout this paper we treat LegitScript the same as NABP and label websites certified by either agency as NABP-certified.

The other two private certifiers – PharmacyChecker.com and the Canadian International Pharmacy Association (CIPA) – are fundamentally different from NABP/LegitScript. CIPA is a trade association of Canadian pharmacies and only certifies Canadian websites that comply with Canadian laws, while PharmacyChecker.com covers US, Canada, and many other countries. Upon voluntary application (with a fee), PharmacyChecker certifies that any approved website has a valid pharmacy license from its local pharmacy board, requires a prescription for US purchase if the FDA requires a prescription for the medication, protects consumer information, encrypts financial and personal information, and presents a valid mailing address and phone number for contact information. As of

---

[13]See http://www.fda.gov/ICECI/ComplianceManuals/RegulatoryProceduresManual/ucm179266.htm. The FDA defines personal shipments as containing no more than 90-days supply for personal use and does not involve a controlled substance. A controlled substance is a drug that has a high potential for abuse, does not have an accepted medical use, and/or does not meet accepted safety requirements.

[14]LegitScript was founded by a former White House aide named John Horton.

March 9, 2012, PharmacyChecker has approved 73 foreign websites and 51 US websites. PharmacyChecker also charges fees for an approved website to be listed on PharmacyChecker.com beyond a short period of initial approval. Consequently, those listed on PharmacyChecker's Pharmacy Ratings page are only a selected list of PharmacyChecker-approved websites. Because PharmacyChecker is unwilling to share their complete list of approvals, we are not able to conduct a full comparison between approvals by PharmacyChecker and those by the NABP, LegitScript or the CIPA. Of the 37 websites listed on the Pharmacy Ratings page of PharmacyChecker.com, only three are labeled US while all the others are either listed under one foreign country or a number of foreign countries plus US. This list is incompletely overlapped with the list of approval from the NABP, LegitScript and the CIPA. Among the four certification agencies, PharmacyChecker is the only one that provides head-to-head drug price comparison across online pharmacies.

As detailed in the next subsection, Google used to contract with PharmacyChecker to filter websites listed in its sponsored search page but switched to NABP/LegitScript after it agreed to ban non-NABP-certified pharmacies in February 2010.

Before we focus on the Google policy regarding online pharmacies, it is important to understand why US consumers buy prescription drugs online. According to Gurau (2005), the most frequent reasons quoted by interviewees for buying or intending to buy online were convenience and saving money, followed by information anonymity and choice. Skinner (2005) estimated that Canadian prices for the 100 top-selling brand-name drugs were on average 43% below US prices for the same drugs.[15] Quon et al. (2005) compared 12 Canadian Internet pharmacies with 3 major online US drug chain pharmacies and found that Americans can save an average of approximately 24% per unit of drug on the 44 most-commonly purchased brand-name medications from Canada. In an audit study, Bate, Jin and Mathur (2013) purchased samples of five popular brand-name prescription drugs from NABP/LegitScript-certified websites (tier-A), PharmacyChecker/CIPA-certified websites (tier-B), and websites that were not certified by any of the four certifiers (tier-C). After comparing the purchased samples with authentic versions, they found similar drug quality between tier-A and tier-B samples, but the cash price of tier-B samples were 49.2% cheaper than tier-A samples after controlling for other factors.[16] These findings suggest that a lower price for brand-name prescription drugs is an important incentive for US consumers to shop online.

As for what type of drugs are purchased online, Fox (2004) reported that the most frequently bought drugs were for chronic conditions (75%), followed by weight loss and sexual performance substances (25%). Consistently, Skinner (2006) found resemblance between the top five therapeutic categories used by US seniors and the top five therapeutic categories in the cross-border online sales from Canada to US. This suggests that seniors are an important source of demand for Canadian pharmacies. Bate, Jin and Mathur (2013) reported an online survey of RxRights members. Because

---

[15]This number has adjusted for currency equivalency. Skinner (2005) also reported that the 100 top-selling generic drugs are on average priced 78% higher in Canada than in the US. This explains why most cross-border sales from Canada to US concentrated on brand-name drugs.

[16]The price difference was mostly driven by non-Viagra drugs. There was no significant price difference across tiers for Viagra.

RxRights is a non-profit organization that pays attention to the cost of prescription drugs, their members are likely more price sensitive than the general population. Among 2,907 respondents who purchase prescription medication for either themselves or family members, 54.8% admitted to purchasing at least one category of the drugs online at some time in the past year, 72.4% of online shoppers purchased from foreign websites only, and an overwhelming majority (91.1%) cited cost savings to be one of the reasons for buying from foreign websites. Surprisingly, most respondents had medical insurance and/or some prescription drug coverage, and the percentage of being insured was not lower among online shoppers. Comments left by respondents suggested that incomplete coverage on prescription drugs, in the form of high deductible, high coinsurance rate, or the donut hole of the Medicare Part D coverage, was one of the factors that motivated the insured to shop online. The survey reported in Bate, Jin and Mathur (2013) also highlighted how respondents searched for pharmacies. Conditional on shopping online, 53.1% used Internet search, 40.4% checked with a credentialing agency such as PharmacyChecker, 22.4% used personal referrals, and only 12.7% looked for the cheapest deal. Consistently, most online shoppers restrict themselves to one primary website, sometimes with supplements from other websites.

2.2 Google Policy on Online Pharmacies

As summarized in Table 1, Google used to contract with PharmacyChecker to ensure that every pharmacy website listed in Google's sponsored search page is legitimate according to PharmacyChecker's certification standard. Despite this policy, the FDA found in July 2009 that some online pharmacies advertising on Google had not been approved by PharmacyChecker.[17] Shortly after (November 2009), the FDA issued 22 warning letters to website operators.[18] At about the same time (August 2009), a study published by LegitScript.com and KnuhOn.com criticized Microsoft Bing for allowing rogue online pharmacy to advertise on its search engine. The study found that "89.7% (of the advertising websites) led to 'rogue' Internet pharmacies that do not require a prescription for prescription drugs, or are otherwise acting unlawfully or fraudulently."[19] While 89.7% is an impressive number, one should note that LegitScript will "not approve websites sourcing prescription drugs in a way that the FDA has indicated is contrary to US law (meaning, 'Canadian' or other foreign pharmacy websites)."[20] In contrast, PharmacyChecker certifies some foreign pharmacies that would not be certified by LegitScript.

Figure 1 presents a screen shot of Google search page following the query "Liptor" in 2008. On the left hand side are organic links featured by brand-name website (lipitor.com) and information oriented websites such as wikipedia.org. On the right hand side are sponsor links, the top two of

---

[17]http://www.nytimes.com/2011/05/14/technology/14google.html?_r=0.

[18]http://www.fda.gov/NewsEvents/Newsroom/PressAnnouncements/ucm191330.htm. The current FDA website hosting safety information of online purchase of drugs: http://www.fda.gov/Drugs/ResourcesForYou/Consumers/BuyingUsingMedicineSafely/BuyingMedicinesOvertheInternet/default.htm.

[19]The report http://www.cnn.com/2009/TECH/08/20/internet.drugs/index.html posts the link http://www.legitscript.com/BingRxReport.pdf, but it is unavailable to access on December 25, 2012. The report is also available here: http://www.legitscript.com/download/BingRxReport.pdf.

[20]http://www.legitscript.com/services/certification.

them are clearly foreign pharmacies (canadapharmacy.com and canadadrugpharmacy.com). The manufacturer (Pfizer) also placed a sponsored link of lipitor.com at the top of the whole page.

In response to the highlighted concern of drug safety, on February 9, 2010, Google announced two changes regarding its pharmacy advertising policy. The first change is to only accept ads from US online pharmacy websites that are certified by the NABP and from Canadian websites that are certified by CIPA. The second change is that the NABP-certified websites can only target their ads to Google users in the US and the CIPA-certified websites can only target Google users in Canada. The new policy is only applicable to US and Canada.[21] Two months later (April 21, 2010), LegitScript announced assistance to Google in implementing Google's Internet pharmacy advertising policy in place of PharmacyChecker.[22] On June 10, 2010, both Microsoft and Yahoo! started to require NABP certification for online pharmacy advertisers.[23]

In May 2011, Google announced in its quarterly report that "in connection with ... an investigation by the United States Department of Justice into the use of Google advertising by certain advertisers, we accrued $500 million for the three month period ended March 31, 2011."[24] On August 24, 2011, the DOJ made it official that "Google Forfeits $500 Million Generated by Online Ads & Prescription Drug Sales by Canadian Online Pharmacies." The press release states that "Under the terms of an agreement signed by Google and the government, Google acknowledges that it improperly assisted Canadian online pharmacy advertisers to run advertisements that targeted the United States ..."[25]

Figure 2 presents a screen shot of Google search page following the query "lipitor" in 2013. In contrast to Figure 1, there are no sponsored links on the page except for lipitor.com at the top. The void of sponsored search on the right hand side is filled by a drug fact label of lipitor with links to official information about the drug's side effects, warnings and user guidance from the National Library of Medicine. The drug fact label started on June 22, 2010 under a partnership between Google and the National Institute of Health (NIH)[26], and probably has diverted some click traffic following drug name queries after the ban.

In light of these events, we define three regimes for our empirical analysis as shown in Table 2. Regime 0 refers to a 17-month period up to January 2010, right before Google adopted the ban. Regime 1 ranges from March 2010 to July 2011, covering a period after the Google ban but before the Google-DOJ settlement. The 13-month period after the Google-DOJ settlement is referred to as Regime 2. Because our data are monthly but both the Google ban and the Google-DOJ settlement occurred in the middle of a month, our sample excludes the two event months (February 2010 and August 2011). As mentioned in Section 1, we classify pharmacy websites into three tiers: tier-A refers to NABP/LegitScript-certified US websites that are always allowed to advertise in Google sponsored search. Tier-B refers to the pharmacy websites that are not certified by NABP/LegitScript, but

---

[21] http://adwords.blogspot.com/2010/02/update-to-pharmacy-policy-in-us-and.html.
[22] http://blog.legitscript.com/2010/04/legitscript-to-help-google-implement-internet-pharmacy-ad-policy/.
[23] https://www.nabp.net/news/microsoft-and-yahoo-now-require-vipps-accreditation-for-online-pharmacy-advertise
[24] http://sec.gov/Archives/edgar/data/1288776/000119312511134428/d10q.htm, .
[25] http://www.justice.gov/opa/pr/2011/August/11-dag-1078.html.
[26] http://venturebeat.com/2010/06/22/google-health-search-adds-drug-info-upping-pharma-ad-spend/.

certified by PharmacyChecker or CIPA. All the pharmacy websites that are not certified by any of the four certification agencies are referred to as tier-C. By definition, only tier-C websites were blocked (imperfectly) from sponsored listings in regime 0, whereas both tier-B and tier-C websites are blocked in regime 1 and regime 2. Throughout the paper, we use "NABP-certified" exchangeably with "tier-A", "other-certified" exchangeably with "tier-B", and "uncertified" exchangeably with "tier-C".

3 Conceptual and Econometric Framework

While consumers have many ways to reach drug-related websites, here we focus on searches through search engines due to data limitations. For simplicity, this section assumes that there is only one search engine available and therefore abstracts from substitution between search engines.[27] Conditional on a consumer using a search engine, her search consists of entering a query in the search box and clicking into website link(s) offered in the search results page.[28] As detailed below, most clicks into pharmacy sites come from queries related to pharmacies (e.g., canadapharmacy, pharmacychecker, or "cheap drug Canada"), queries containing a drug name (e.g., lipitor), or queries related to health conditions, drug manufacturers, drug regulators, etc. Organic and paid clicks are recorded separately in the comScore data. To examine how paid, organic or total clicks change after the ban, we assess the effects on both the extensive and intensive margins using a two-part model.[29] The extensive margin is whether a website receives any positive clicks in a given month,[30] while the the intensive margin is the number of clicks a website receives, conditional on receiving some (non-censored) clicks.

Defining $Y_{it}^{AllQueries}$ as paid/organic/total clicks that website i received in month t, we investigate the extensive margin using a probit regression:

$$Prob(Y_{it}^{AllQueries} > 0) = \Phi(\alpha + \sum_{k \in \{B,C\}} \beta_k * Tier_k + \sum_{r=1}^{2} \gamma_r * Regime_r \quad (1)$$
$$+ \sum_{k \in \{B,C\}} \sum_{r=1}^{2} \theta_{kr} * Tier_k * Regime_r).$$

Tier and *Regime* are indicator variables for the type of pharmacy (tier A, B, or C) accessed at

---

[27] Our data contain search and click volumes for each of the five largest search engines. According to comScore, Google has a 64-67% market share in organic search during our sample period. Because some comScore data on searchers are not engine specific, our empirical results pool all engines.

[28] We use the term "query" to denote the actual text the user enters into the search box on the search engine and the term "click" to denote the subsequent clicks by the user on organic or paid links that result from the search. The data include the number of times a certain query was entered into a search engine and the number of clicks on each link, conditional on the query. A query with no subsequent clicks is recorded by comScore as one query and zero clicks.

[29] The distribution of clicks per website is characterized by a spike at zero and a bell-shape positive distribution skewed to the right, and the two-part model with a log-normal positive distribution best captures the data pattern.

[30] The number of clicks is coded as censored if the website receives too few clicks. We do not have specific information on the censoring rule, so we code the censored clicks as zero. In one specification, we analyze the extensive margin as whether a website receives any positive or censored clicks, and the results are similar.

website i and the time period to which month t belongs (regime 0, 1, or 2).

The intensive margin is assessed using a simple OLS model conditional on a website receiving positive clicks:

$$(ln(Y_{it}^{AllQueries})|Y_{it}^{AllQueries} > 0) = \alpha_i + \sum_{r=1}^{2} \gamma_r * Regime_r \qquad (2)$$
$$+ \sum_{k \in \{B,C\}} \sum_{r=1}^{2} \theta_{kr} * Tier_k * Regime_r + \epsilon_{it},$$

where α_i denotes website fixed effects. Because website fixed effects absorb the tier dummies, $Tier_k$ only appears in the interaction with $Regime_r$. We do not include website fixed effects in equation (1) because a probit regression with fixed effects may introduce an incidental parameter problem. In both specifications (1) and (2), θ_{kr} measures the conditional differential effect of regime 1 and regime 2 for tier-B and tier-C websites compared with the control group tier-A pharmacies in regime 0.

A priori, when total organic and paid clicks are the dependent variable, one may expect θ_{kr} to be negative for tier-B and tier-C websites after the ban, either because the ban has sent a negative message about the safety of these websites or because the ban has made it more difficult to find tier-B and tier-C sites even if consumers' beliefs remain unchanged. The challenge is how to distinguish these two explanations. One strategy is to explore the timing difference: arguably, the massive media coverage on the Google-DOJ settlement (regime 2) may have increased the salience of the negative message about the safety of tier-B and tier-C websites, while the difficulty to find these websites should have increased in regime 1, right after Google started to ban these websites from sponsored search. Moving from regime 1 to regime 2, consumers' perceptions about the safety of tier-B and tier-C sites may have been affected by the settlement. This suggests that we can differentiate the above two explanations by comparing the effects of the ban in regime 1 and regime 2.

The second strategy is to compare the changes in total and organic clicks on tier-B and tier-C websites. Because tier-C websites were prohibited from sponsored listings even before the ban[31], the ban should be a greater shock to clicks on tier-B websites than on tier-C websites, if the main effect of the ban is informing consumers of the danger of other-certified websites. This implies that the organic clicks on tier-B websites should drop more after the ban than those on tier-C websites. In contrast, if the main effect of the ban is adding consumer search cost in reaching non-NABP-certified websites, the drop in the organic clicks on tier-B websites may be smaller than those on tier-C websites, either because tier-B websites were on average easier to find in organic search (proxied by their organic clicks before the ban) or because tier-B websites were perceived safer than tier-C websites thanks to their non-NABP certification.

The above regressions summarize all search behaviors including what query to search for and

---

[31] Paid clicks are observed on tier-C websites due to imperfect screening by the search engines.

what link to click into. Assuming the ban has different effects on tier-B and tier-C pharmacy sites (which turns out to be true in our data), we can further examine which consumer behavior leads to the difference: is it because the ban motivates differential search intensity on pharmacy queries that spell out the names of tier-B or tier-C sites, or because searchers are more or less likely to click into tier-B or tier-C sites conditional on the same pharmacy queries? Taking tier-A pharmacy name queries as the baseline, the effect on query intensity can be studied in the following specification:

$$ln(Y_{jt}^{Pharmacy}) = \alpha_j^P + \alpha_t^P + \beta_1^P \cdot X_j^P \cdot Regime_1 + \beta_2^P \cdot X_j^P \cdot Regime_2 + \epsilon_{jt}^P, \tag{3}$$

where $Y_{jt}^{Pharmacy}$ denotes the number of searches for pharmacy query j in month t.[32] X_j is a set of dummies indicating the type of query j. The coefficients $\{\beta_1^P, \beta_2^P\}$ denote the difference-in-differences estimates of how the two regimes affect various pharmacy queries as compared to the queries on tier-A pharmacy names.

As detailed in Section 4.2, we can distinguish pharmacy name queries (e.g. "cvs"), discount pharmacy queries (e.g. "cheap drug") and general pharmacy queries (e.g. "pharmacy at"). Different pharmacy query types may indicate different intentions to search and therefore we expect a different response to the ban. To capture the effect of the ban on clicks into website i conditional on pharmacy query type j, let X_j be the dummy variable for each pharmacy query type. We extend equations (1) and (2) to allow the key parameters, $\{\gamma_r, \theta_{kr}\}$, to vary by the type of query:

$$\begin{aligned} Prob(Y_{ijt}^{Pharmacy} > 0)) &= \Phi(\sum_j \alpha_j X_j + \sum_{k \in \{B,C\}} Tier_k + \sum_{r=1}^{2} Regime_r \\ &+ \sum_j \sum_{k \in \{B,C\}} \beta_{kj} Tier_k * X_j + + \sum_j \sum_{r=1}^{2} \gamma_{rj} Regime_r * X_j \\ &+ \sum_j \sum_{k \in \{B,C\}} \sum_{r=1}^{2} \theta_{krj} * Tier_k * Regime_r * X_j), \end{aligned} \tag{4}$$

$$\begin{aligned} ln(Y_{ijt}^{Pharmacy} | Y_{ijt}^{Pharmacy} > 0) &= \sum_j \alpha_j * X_j + \sum_{r=1}^{2} Regime_r \\ &+ \sum_j \sum_{k \in \{B,C\}} \beta_{kj} Tier_k * X_j + + \sum_j \sum_{r=1}^{2} \gamma_{rj} Regime_r * X_j \\ &+ \sum_j \sum_{k \in \{B,C\}} \sum_{r=1}^{2} \theta_{krj} * Tier_k * Regime_r + \epsilon_{ijt}. \end{aligned} \tag{5}$$

The relationship between a user's query and resulting click destinations sheds light on the economic effects of the ban. If a query for "discount pharmacy" directs more traffic away from both

---

[32] We also estimate equation 3 using the number of searchers that submit query j in month t.

tier-B and tier-C websites after the ban, it suggests that consumers have heightened safety concerns for all non-NABP-certified websites. In comparison, if the query directs traffic away from tier-C sites but not from tier-B sites, it is probably because consumers are willing to tolerate the risk of tier-B sites and/or find a way to get around the ban of tier-B sites in sponsored search. Pharmacy name queries provide more direct evidence. If we find a tier-C pharmacy name query leads to fewer organic clicks on tier-C sites but a tier-B pharmacy name query does not lead to fewer organic clicks on tier-B sites, one explanation is that the ban has different effects in conveying the safety risk for these two types of pharmacy sites. Search cost is less able to explain this data pattern because both tier-B and tier-C sites are highly ranked in organic search results if we search for their pharmacy names directly.

We also explore how the effect of the ban differs by the types of drugs consumers search for on the Internet. Existing literature suggests that consumers that target chronic or privacy-oriented drugs will be affected the most by the ban because cost saving and privacy are dominant reasons for using online/foreign pharmacies before the ban. The Oxford English Dictionary defines a lifestyle drug as "a drug prescribed to treat a condition that is not necessarily serious or life-threatening but that has a significant impact on the quality of life."[33] While this definition does not explicitly identify a specific set of drugs, we evaluate how the ban's effect varies for drugs that usually treat less serious conditions (e.g., drugs that target erectile dysfunction and smoking cessation). The demand for these drugs may be more price-elastic than drugs that treat life-threatening conditions.[34] Non-NABP-certified websites may be more attractive for lifestyle drugs, either because users of these drugs appreciate privacy or because they do not have a formal prescription and prefer websites with a less rigid prescription requirement.

However, as the ban cannot prohibit consumers from reaching non-NABP-certified pharmacies via organic links, it is unclear whether the ban leads to more or less of a click reduction for these drug queries. To examine this question, we classify drug queries according to (1) whether drug query j attracted a high fraction of clicks into non-NABP-certified pharmacies before the ban, (2) whether drug query j targets lifestyle drugs or controlled substances, and (3) whether drug query j targets chronic drugs.[35] Defining each classification variable as X_{g_j}, we estimate the differential effects of the ban on the extensive margin of clicks into pharmacy site i from drug query type g_j in

---

[33] See http://www.oed.com/view/Entry/108129. In addition, one medical article by Gilbert, Wally and New in the *British Medical Journal*, describes a drug in this category as "one used for 'non-health' problems or for problems that lie at the margins of health and well being."

[34] Of course, some lifestyle drugs are at times used to treat serious medical conditions.

[35] For robustness, we also considered drugs for whom the searchers were more likely to be elderly or low-income before the ban.

month t (Y_{ijt}), by:

$$Prob(Y_{igt}^{Drug} > 0)) = \Phi(\sum_g \alpha_g X_g + \sum_{k \in \{B,C\}} Tier_k + \sum_{r=1}^{2} Regime_r \quad (6)$$

$$+ \sum_g \sum_{k \in \{B,C\}} \beta_{kg} Tier_k * X_g + + \sum_g \sum_{r=1}^{2} \gamma_{rg} Regime_r * X_g$$

$$+ \sum_g \sum_{k \in \{B,C\}} \sum_{r=1}^{2} \theta_{krg} * Tier_k * Regime_r * X_g,$$

$$ln(Y_{igt}^{Drug} | Y_{igt}^{Drug} > 0) = \sum_g \alpha_g * X_g + \sum_{r=1}^{2} Regime_r \quad (7)$$

$$+ \sum_g \sum_{k \in \{B,C\}} \beta_{kg} Tier_k * X_g + + \sum_g \sum_{r=1}^{2} \gamma_{rg} Regime_r * X_g$$

$$+ \sum_g \sum_{k \in \{B,C\}} \sum_{r=1}^{2} \theta_{krg} * Tier_k * Regime_r + \epsilon_{igt}.$$

The coefficients of the interaction terms with X_{g_j}, denoted as $\{\gamma_{rg}, \theta_{krg}\}$, indicate whether the ban has differential effects on clicks by the type of drug query.

4 Data Summary

Our primary datasource is comScore.[36] ComScore tracks the online activity of over two million persons worldwide, one million of whom reside in the US. ComScore extrapolates the observed activity in the households it tracks and by using various demographic weights, it determines the aggregate activity of all US Internet users. We obtained access to click-through data from US households. ComScore data have been used to study internet search behavior by a number of economists including Chen and Waldfogel (2006), Chiou and Tucker (2011), and George and Hogendorn (2013).

4.1 Click and Search Data

We use data from comScore's Search Planner suite of tools, which provides click-through data on queries submitted to five large search engines - Google, Yahoo!, Bing, Ask, and AOL. The click data (available on comScore's "term destinations" report) are organized by query-month-engine and include the number of queries (searches), searchers, and clicks in a given month. In addition, clicks are also broken down into organic versus paid and by destination URL.[37] At times, due to

---

[36] http://www.comscore.com/.
[37] A query is the actual text that a searcher enters on a search engine. Our data include click activity on websites following the exact query, but also clicks following queries where the text appears somewhere in the search box,

small sampling of some queries, click activity is censored because comScore is unable to reliably extrapolate the observed activity to the whole population.[38] We observe 49 months of data from September 2008 to September 2012.

In addition to click activity following each query, we also download from comScore a demographic profile (comScore's "term profile" report) of searchers who perform each query in each month. The profile includes a distribution of age, income, household size, the presence of children, and the geographic location of the searchers. We also observe the share of clicks following a query that are received by each of the five search engines.

Figure 3 shows an example of these reports for Lipitor in January 2012. The term destination report lists the total clicks, divided between organic and paid, following queries for Lipitor in January 2012. Because we selected "match all forms", the click counts include queries for Lipitor alone as well as Lipitor plus other keywords. This report shows clicks on all five search engines combined, but separate reports were also run on individual search engines. The click counts under the key metrics section is comScore's estimate of the total number of clicks by users in the US on all websites following the query. In addition, the clicks are broken down by specific entity.[39] Each entity name is also assigned to one or more categories, such as, health, government, or pharmacy. It is important to note that the clicks we observe on an entity all originate from a search engine. We do not know how many clicks a website receives via direct navigation, bookmarks, etc.

In addition, the term profile report provides information about searchers for Lipitor in January 2012. While the report is not engine-specific, it provides the total number of searches and searchers, irrespective of clicks following those searches. The report also provides demographic information on the households that searched for Lipitor in January 2012. A few examples are shown in the table, but demographics are provided for age, income, geographic region, location (home/work/school), household size, and the presence of children. Finally, the report tells us the share of searches on each of the five search engines.[40]

4.2 Query List and Website Classification

A list of queries must be submitted to comScore in order to extract query-level data. To create a list of drug and pharmacy related terms, we use several resources. The first one is a list of brand names from the FDA's Orange Book of all approved drugs.[41] The second resource is a list of drug

---

potentially along with other words. Plural forms of the query are also included. comScore refers to this as "match-all-forms" queries as opposed to "exact" queries that return the clicks on the query text exactly as entered on the search engine.

[38] Our data has a limitation in regard to censoring. When a click count is censored by comScore, the name of the website entity appears in the database with a click count of -1. This means there were positive clicks on the website during that month, but extrapolation to the population would not produce a reliable estimate. We treat these websites as having zero clicks in our analysis.

[39] Usually an entity name is a URL, but comScore also aggregates clicks on websites with common ownership and lists them under a different entity level (e.g., property, media title, channel, etc). We collect click data at the finest level available to avoid double counting.

[40] From the share, we can determine the number of searches that were performed on each engine, however the demographics are only available for searchers across all engines.

[41] http://www.accessdata.fda.gov/scripts/cder/ob/default.cfm.

manufacturers from Kantar Media[42] We also include three government website names that provide drug information (FDA, NIH, and CDC), and four website names that certify online pharmacies (NABP, LegitScript, PharmacyChecker, and CIPA). The resulting list of queries is supplemented by the names of online pharmacies, which is based on comScore's own categorization of the websites in their data. Running our list of drug names on comScore, we can identify the top pharmacy website names in the comScore "Pharmacy" category.[43] This list, plus any pharmacy names that we can find on any of the four certifying websites, comprise our preliminary list of pharmacy websites.

To address the possibility that searchers may reach drug and pharmacy related websites by searching for a medical condition, symptom, or another non-drug and non-pharmacy term, we supplement the query list with data from Keywordspy.com. This website collects information on keywords that companies bid on for sponsored ads on a search engine. It also reports a list of keywords that more likely lead to organic clicks on a certain website.[44] This allows us to identify a list of organic keywords that are popular searches when the destination is ultimately an online pharmacy. We also add all keywords that the FDA bid on to appear in an engine's sponsored ads.

The combination of all these sources led to over 8,000 queries, far too many to download from comScore given time constraints. Therefore, we restricted the list of drugs to only those that were advertised (in the Kantar media data) and/or prescribed by a physician from 2006-2009.[45] We also ran the complete list of queries through comScore twice on two time windows in 2009 and 2012 and restricted our sample to queries that accounted for the top 90% of clicks in either window. This left us with 690 queries. Because comScore reports the clicks both for the query exactly as it appears and variations of the query (e.g., clicks following a search for "canada online pharmacy" are included in a search for "canada pharmacy"), we only use queries that are not variations of another to avoid double counting. This further restricts our sample to 528 queries. Each query was then submitted to comScore and monthly reports from each search engine were downloaded for the analysis.

Each of the 528 queries are then classified into different query types (see Table 3). Along with drug queries, pharmacy queries are further classified according to their certify-status (tier A, B, or C) as well as general and discount pharmacy keywords. Queries that are not drug or pharmacy related are classified as other.

Table 3 shows the total query count in each category of query. Within each broad group of queries (drug, pharmacy, and other), we further classify the queries by their intention to search for online pharmacies. We expect that the effect of the ban will be most significant on the searches and clicks of queries that are used to reach non-tier-A online pharmacies before the ban. In particular, for the pharmacy query group, we first separate out the queries that are the exact name of the online pharmacy websites and classify them according to the pharmacy tiers. Queries that target pharmacies that sell cheap or discount drugs, and those operate in foreign countries, which more

---

[42]http://kantarmediana.com/intelligence.

[43]The "Pharmacy" category ID on comScore is 778268. A website may have multiple classifications, but any site with this ID we classify as a pharmacy.

[44]This is similar to the Keyword Tool in Google's Adwords.

[45]The latter comes from the National Ambulatory Medical Care Survey (NAMCS).

likely lead to clicks on non-tier-A pharmacies, are classified into discount pharmacy search terms.[46] The remaining pharmacy queries are all general search terms for pharmacies.[47] As discussed in the previous section, the sample of queries in our study are chosen if they lead to a sufficient volume of traffic that can be captured by comScore. Among 528 queries, we choose to focus on drug and pharmacy queries because they are more likely to lead to online pharmacy websites and thus better reflect the changes in consumer search behavior.[48] Figure 4 shows that the number of searchers and searches evolve similarly by broad query groups. Pharmacy search queries experience a spike in the last few months of each year because some pharmacy queries include large retail stores (e.g., walmart and target) with seasonal demand. We control for seasonality in robustness checks of our results.

The last step in processing the data is to classify the destination websites in the database into various categories. We analyze the click data only for pharmacy websites so we classify online pharmacy websites according to their certify-status (tier A, B, or C).[49] The destination website classification is used in the results shown in the regression tables.

Because some of the comScore data are not engine specific, all empirical results present below pool data from all five search engines.

5 Empirical Results

5.1 Descriptive Statistics

Table 4 summarizes the number of searches and clicks by query type. The ratio of online pharmacy clicks to searches (column 3) is associated with the search cost of finding a certain website. If the desired pharmacies do not appear in the paid links or high in the organic results, this may lead consumers to not click on any website and subsequently this would result in a low pharmacy clicks-to-searches ratio.

The ratio of pharmacy clicks to total clicks (column 4) show how paid and organic clicks vary on each type of pharmacies led from different query types. Pharmacy queries lead to many more clicks on pharmacy websites than drug queries. Tier-B names are very likely to lead to pharmacy websites

---

[46] Among 46 discount pharmacy queries, 11 contain the words "canada", "international" and "europe", 5 contain word "online", and 17 contain words "cheap", "discount", "low cost", "free", "deal", and "coupon".

[47] In the general pharmacy terms, there are three queries "pharmacy in", "pharmacy on" and "the pharmacy" carrying exactly the same observations, so we dropped the first two. To check if "the pharmacy" counts all clicks from the query that contains only the word "pharmacy", we calculate the total number of clicks by all queries with "pharmacy" in it except for "the pharmacy". We find that "the pharmacy" always records a larger number of clicks and conclude that "the pharmacy" includes all clicks for queries with "pharmacy" in it. We kept the query "the pharmacy", but subtract the from it the total number of clicks by queries containing the complete word "pharmacy".

[48] In regime 0, only 2.3% of the clicks on pharmacy websites followed queries that were not drug or pharmacy queries, so we choose to not to focus on these queries.

[49] Since the search engine ban only applies to online pharmacies that sell prescription drugs, our analysis is restricted to this set of pharmacies. We cannot directly infer whether a pharmacy sells prescription drugs from its site name or comScore classification, so we check by clicking into each pharmacy website to verify that prescription drugs are sold on the website at the time of our study.

(93-98%) followed by tier-A names (78-81%) and discount pharmacy keywords (59-67%).[50] Tier-C pharmacy names are associated with the lowest percentage of pharmacy clicks among all pharmacy name queries and this percentage drops sharply from 39.8% in regime 0 to 31.4% in regime 1 and 7.1% in regime 2. In contrast, the percentage of pharmacy clicks is stable or even increasing for Tier-B pharmacy names after the ban. Compared with pharmacy queries, drug queries have a much lower percentage of pharmacy clicks (22.1%) and that percentage plummets after the ban (to 2-4%). This is probably because many drug queries target information websites rather than pharmacies and the searchers targeting a pharmacy website using a drug query cannot find the pharmacy sites via sponsored links following the ban. The remaining columns of Table 4 report paid and organic clicks separately. The organic clicks to Tier-B and Tier-C sites have increased after the ban for almost all pharmacy and drug queries, suggesting substitution to organic results when sponsored links are no longer available.

Focusing on pharmacy websites, table 5 also summarizes the organic and paid click volume on pharmacy websites by tier and by regime. For tier-A pharmacies, the number of organic and paid clicks grows from regime 0 to regime 2. Tier-B pharmacies in regime 0 are accessed mostly via paid clicks, with an average of 6,338 monthly paid clicks and 1,795 monthly organic clicks. The ban results in almost 100% loss in paid clicks, but part of the loss is offset by a large increase in organic clicks, suggesting that searchers are substituting organic for paid links. For tier-C websites, the average number of paid clicks falls as expected and the average organic clicks rises in regime 1, but then falls in regime 2, consistent with substitution to organic links in regime 1 and more awareness of the risks associated with these sites in regime 2. The differential change in organic clicks on tier-B and tier-C websites is evident in Figure 5, where we plot the monthly trends of paid and organic clicks by tier. Part of the reduction in organic clicks on tier-C pharmacies may be attributable to fewer tier-C pharmacy queries after the ban, as shown in Figure 6.

The last three columns of Table 5 show the distribution of number of websites active in each regime. With the same set of queries in each regime, the number of online pharmacy websites that are recorded as having any clicks in comScore is relatively stable for tier-A and tier-B pharmacies, but declines 33% for tier-C from 138 to 92. This decline could be due to both health concerns and search costs. The decline in the number of tier-C websites may have several implications. For pharmacy competition, this may benefit the remaining tier-C pharmacies if consumers preferring tier-C pharmacies continue to buy from them. However, if consumers are shifting from tier-C to tier-B or tier-A pharmacies, we will observe clicks on tier-C websites decline as a whole.

The top panel of table A1 in the appendix lists examples of drug queries that led to a high proportion of clicks into tier-B and tier-C websites in the first 9 months of our sample (September 2008 to May 2009) before the ban. Five of the top 10 drug queries on list are controlled substances. The bottom panel lists drugs with a low proportion of clicks into tier-B and tier-C websites. Only one query in the tier-B list is controlled substance and it also includes more drugs that target

---

[50]The average clicks per search and the percent pharmacy clicks are first calculated at the query level and then averaged.

chronic diseases such as high blood pressure. These patterns are not surprising as tier-C sites are less likely to require prescriptions and controlled substances are subject to closer screening by the FDA at customs enforcement. In an unreported table, we also rank drug queries by the absolute count of total clicks into tier-B or tier-C sites. These alternative ranks are similar to the ranks presented in Table A1, except that some high-volume drug queries are ranked higher in the tier-B list if they target chronic conditions (e.g., lipitor and insulin) or ranked higher in the tier-C list if they target lifestyle drugs or controlled substances.

Overall, these statistics suggest a similar trend in searches across broad query groups, but different click patterns into tier-A, tier-B and tier-C websites. In general, we observe more paid and organic clicks on tier-A pharmacies, a greater substitution from paid clicks to organic clicks for tier-B pharmacies after the ban, a reduction in organic clicks for tier-C pharmacies as well as a reduction in search intensity for tier-C pharmacy names. The drug queries that led to tier-B and tier-C clicks before the ban are also different: tier-B sites were more likely to receive clicks from searches for chronic drugs, while tier-C sites were more likely to receive clicks from queries for lifestyle drugs or controlled substances.

5.2 Regression Results

5.2.1 Total Clicks from All Queries

Our first set of regressions focus on clicks received by pharmacy website i in month t from all queries. As detailed in Section 3, this is our broadest specification and it summarizes all search behavior leading to pharmacy websites.

Table 6 reports pharmacy website results for total and organic clicks. Within total clicks, column (1) examines whether website i received any clicks in month t; Column (2) examines whether website i received any positive clicks in month t, where positive clicks refers to non-censored click counts in the comScore data. Both columns (1) and (2) refer to the extensive margin, following the probit specification in equation (1). On the intensive margin, column (3) uses equation (2) to examine the log of the number of clicks, conditional on a website receiving positive clicks in the month. Because click traffic of many websites is too low to have non-censored positive clicks, the number of observations drops 72% from columns (1) and (2) to column (3). The results for "any click" and "any positive click" are similar, so for organic clicks we only report regressions for "any positive organic click" (column 4) and log positive organic clicks conditional on having positive organic clicks (column 5). All columns use tier-A sites as the excluded baseline group.

The first three columns suggest that, after the ban, tier-C sites suffer on the extensive margin while tier-B sites suffer on the intensive margin. In particular, the probability of a tier-C site receiving any positive clicks falls 6.69 percentage points in regime 1 and the net effect grows to 10.92 percentage points by regime 2. In comparison, there is no significant change in the probability of a tier-B site receiving any positive click. Conditional on receiving any positive clicks, the amount of total clicks received by a tier-B site falls 61.7% in regime 1 and by a similar magnitude (58.3%) in regime 2. Recall that the ban on sponsored search was effective in both regimes 1 and 2, but the Google-DOJ settlement at the beginning of regime 2 had broader media coverage and likely heightened the health concerns of uncertified pharmacies. The larger drop in tier-C clicks in regime 2, together with the lack of a further drop of tier-B clicks in regime 2, suggests that consumers may have had more health concerns with tier-C sites than with tier-B sites after the Google-DOJ settlement. Another possible explanation is that tier-C websites were ranked low in organic results and their organic ranks became even lower in regime 2 as consumers had difficulty finding them in regime 1.

Focusing on organic clicks only, the last two columns of Table 6 show that tier-B sites enjoy an 88.2% increase of organic clicks in regime 1 from regime 0 and 113.6% increase in regime 2 relative to tier-A. Combined with the fall in total clicks on these sites, this suggests that the loss of paid clicks on tier-B sites was offset with an increase in organic clicks, although total clicks still fall. In contrast, tier-C sites suffer a reduction in traffic via both organic and total clicks, and the reduction is greater in regime 2 than in regime 1. These differential effects suggest that the ban generates search frustration and some, but not all, consumers switch from paid to organic links for tier-B sites. This does not rule out health concerns for tier-B sites, but the Google-DOJ settlement may have raised more health concerns for tier-C sites than for tier-B sites.

We also estimate auxiliary models to assess the robustness of these results. To control for the possibility of a pre-treatment trend in clicks, we include a trend term that was allowed to vary separately in each regime. We also checked for the impact of seasonality by including a dummy variable for the holiday months of November and December for tier-A sites. Neither of these specifications impacted the qualitative results.[51] Because the ban on tier-B and tier-C pharmacies from sponsored links was imperfect (as shown in figure 5), we also conducted robustness checks on the cut-off date of regime 1 (the date of the ban) in two ways. First, we used a new regime 1 cut-off corresponding to the actual month when paid clicks on non-NABP certified pharmacies fell to nearly zero (September 2010). Second, we performed a placebo check by placing the regime cut-off in June 2009, well before the ban. The first strategy does not affect the qualitative results and the second shows no change in organic and paid clicks in the hypothetical regime 1 treatment period before the actual ban. In the first strategy, we also tried cutting the regime 1 into two halves corresponding to before and after September 2010. We find the coefficients similar for these two periods, except that the reduction in total clicks on tier-C websites at the extensive margin is deepened relative to tier-A in the second half of regime 1.

5.2.2 A Closer Look at Pharmacy Queries

We next investigate whether the click reduction on tier-B/tier-C sites is driven by consumers searching less intensively for tier-B/tier-C pharmacy names or a lower likelihood to click on tier-B/tier-C sites, conditional on a particular type of pharmacy query. To answer this question, Table 7 reports regressions of log (searchers) and log (searches) of pharmacy queries. Taking tier-A pharmacy queries as the baseline, we look into general pharmacy queries, discount queries, tier-B queries and

---
[51]Estimates for all robustness checks are available from the authors upon request.

tier-C queries separately. The only significant effects in this table are the drop of searches and searchers in tier-C pharmacy queries. The similar magnitudes of the effect on searches and searchers suggest that fewer consumers search for tier-C pharmacy names after the ban and even fewer after the Google-DOJ settlement.

Table 8 examines how the ban changed total clicks into website i from a pharmacy query of type j. We report the extensive margin (total clicks > 0) and the intensive margin (log(total clicks), if positive) separately. Within each margin, we organize columns by destination: $1\times$ denotes the baseline destination (tier-A), tier-B$\times$ denotes additional effects into tier-B destinations, and tier-C$\times$ denotes additional effects into tier-C destinations. The rows are organized by pharmacy query types: general, discount, tier-B and tier-C relative to tier-A queries. The most noticeable result is that tier-B and discount queries more likely lead to tier-B destinations after the ban but a tier-C query is less likely to lead to a tier-C destination. One possible explanation is that tier-B websites appear high in organic ranks when consumers search for the tier-B names but tier-C websites are ranked lower when consumers search for the tier-C names. Although we do not know the exact organic ranks of each result in our sample period, we have searched tier-B and tier-C pharmacy names in Google in 2013 and found the pharmacy websites appear highly ranked in all cases. If the organic results in our sample period are similar to what we observe in 2013, this does not explain the differential effect on tier-B and tier-C queries from our regression. These results, combined with a lower search intensity for tier-C queries, suggest that consumers may shy away from tier-C websites due to health concerns but are persistent in searching for and clicking into tier-B websites despite potentially higher search costs.

5.2.3 Heterogeneous Effects of Drug Queries

Pharmacy queries are often associated with clicks on pharmacy websites, however we do not observe which drug or condition the searchers are interested in once they click on the website. In contrast, each drug query focuses on a particular drug, which allows us to explore heterogeneous effects across different drugs or across different types of searchers.[52]

The existing literature suggests that consumers tend to use online pharmacies for chronic or privacy-sensitive conditions. Foreign online pharmacies can offer large cost savings if a brand name drug is expensive in the US and consumers need it frequently. Some foreign pharmacies, especially those in tier-C, offer online consultation and have less restrictive prescription requirements than pharmacies in other tiers. These features can be attractive to consumers who are reluctant to obtain a prescription because of privacy concerns or because of perceived stigmas associated with some lifestyle drugs. In light of this literature, we explore heterogeneous effects of the ban in four directions.

First, we characterize drugs according to the percentage of clicks before the ban on tier-B or

---

[52] We are not able to explore heterogeneous effects across different types of searchers for pharmacy queries because the search volume on each pharmacy query is not large for comScore to provide searcher demographics both before and after the ban.

tier-C sites. For a particular drug that had non-censored total clicks in the first nine months of our data before the ban (September 2008 to May 2009, a total of 233 drugs), we compute the fraction of total clicks into tier-B and tier-C sites. The distribution of this fraction is very skewed, ranging from 100% (for two queries that only led to tier-C clicks) to 0% (for 110 queries that only led to tier-A clicks). A total of 79 drugs are defined as H-drugs if this fraction is greater than 3%, and 112 drugs are defined as L-drugs if this fraction is below 0.1%.[53] In the regressions for both extensive and intensive margins, we take L-drug queries as the baseline and examine whether H-drug queries have a differential effect on the interactions between the destination tier and regime dummies. The regression sample excludes the first nine months of our data because they are used to define the H and L drugs.

Estimates of equations (6) and (7) are shown in table 9. The results show that H-drug queries are associated with a greater loss in clicks on tier-B or tier-C sites after the ban. Specifically, H-drug queries experience more of a reduction in tier-B and tier-C total clicks on the intensive margin. However, organic clicks for tier-B sites following H-drug queries are unaffected while they fall for tier-C sites.

In contrast to the substitution to organic links following pharmacy queries after the ban, the lack of substitution to organic clicks following H-drug queries is possibly because tier-B sites rarely show up as high-ranked organic links when one searches for a specific drug. In contrast, tier-B sites often appear on the first page of organic results if one enters pharmacy queries. These losses in total and organic clicks on tier-C sites are larger and more significant after the Google-DOJ settlement, which is consistent with the previous finding that consumers shy away from tier-C sites due to not only increased search cost after the ban but also heightened health concerns after the settlement.

Our second analysis of heterogeneous effects focuses on lifestyle drugs, which usually treat less serious or non-life threatening conditions. While this definition does not specify particular drugs or drug classes in this category, in our analysis we define lifestyle drugs as those that target ED (5 queries), birth control (11 queries), weight loss (3 queries), facial skin problems (11 queries), or smoking cessation (3 queries). We also include drugs that are designated as controlled substances by the US government (23 queries).[54] These drugs are by no means a definitive list of lifestyle drugs, but we believe the demand for these drugs may be more price elastic and therefore the effect of the ban may be greater compared to other types of drugs. In total, 50 drug queries are classified as lifestyle drugs.[55] As we expect, lifestyle drug queries are more likely to result in clicks into tier-C sites before the ban.[56] Taking non-lifestyle drug queries as the baseline, Table 10 reports regression results for the differential effects of lifestyle drug queries. In general, the differential effect

---

[53]The other 42 drugs had a fraction of total clicks into tier-B and tier-C sites ranging between 0.1% and 2.72%. We omit these queries in the regressions. Appendix Table A1 provides a list of the top 10 H-drug queries and top 10 L-drug queries, ranked by the total clicks on pharmacy websites.

[54]Some, but not all, sleep aid, ADHD and muscle relaxant drugs are controlled substances.

[55]Appendix Table A2 provides a list of top 10 lifestyle queries and top 10 non-lifestyle queries, ranked by the number of pharmacy-related clicks following each query.

[56]The fraction of total clicks into tier-C sites in the first nine months of our data is 6.9% for lifestyle drug queries, and 2.81% for non-lifestyle drugs.

is insignificant, except for a greater reduction in total clicks from lifestyle queries into tier-B sites on the intensive margin and a greater reduction in total clicks into tier-C sites on the extensive margin, both after the Google-DOJ settlement.

A third type of heterogeneous effect could exist between chronic and non-chronic drug queries. A drug query is defined as chronic if the drug was on average prescribed five or more times a year per patient in the nationally representative 2010 Medical Expenditure Panel Survey (MEPS). A query is defined non-chronic if the average prescription frequency is below 3.5 per patient per year. In total, we have 73 chronic drug queries and 83 non-chronic drug queries.[57] Those with no representation in the MEPS data or with prescription frequency between 3.5 and 5 are dropped from regressions.

Taking non-chronic queries as the baseline, Table 11 shows that chronic queries suffer less of a reduction in total and organic clicks into tier-B and tier-C sites on the intensive margin. These effects are larger and more significant after the Google-DOJ settlement. In comparison, there is no significant differential effect between chronic and non-chronic queries on the extensive margin. Because the intensive margin captures larger websites by definition, this suggests that the ban has less (and in fact close to zero) effect on clicks from chronic queries to large tier-B and tier-C websites. These differential effects are impressive if we consider the facts that the banned pharmacies have a low chance to appear high in organic results following a drug query and the percent of clicks on pharmacy websites following drug queries has plummeted from 22% to 2-3% after the ban.[58]

Our results show that organic and paid clicks on tier-A pharmacies increase after the ban on non-NABP certified pharmacies. Total clicks on tier-B pharmacies fall after the ban, though consumers substitute to organic links to partially offset of the fall in paid clicks. Clicks on tier-C sites fall as well, and we find very little substitution to organic links after the ban. This is consistent with health concerns driving consumers away from non-tier-A pharmacies, though are still willing to click (potentially with higher search costs) on other-certified tier-B sites after their ban. it is also consistent with the possibility that tier-B sites are ranked higher than tier-C sites in organic results and therefore are easier to find when sponsored links disappear from the search page. Our analysis of heterogeneous impacts shows that the effects on tier-B and tier-C websites are larger for H-drugs, lifestyle drugs, and drugs that treat non-chronic conditions.

6 Conclusion

We have shown that following the ban on non-NABP-certified pharmacies from sponsored search, there is a reduction in total clicks into the banned pharmacies. However, this effect is differential in several dimensions.

First, the websites certified by non-NABP agencies – referred to as tier-B sites – experience a

---

[57]Appendix Table A3 provides a list of the top 10 chronic queries and top 10 non-chronic queries ranked by the number of pharmacy-related clicks following each query.

[58]Although we do not present the results here, we also investigated if the average demographics of each drug searcher had a heterogeneous impact on how the ban affected clicks on pharmacy websites. We find that the ban has no differential effect on queries that had on average older searchers or lower-income searchers. These tables are available upon request.

reduction in total clicks, and some of their lost paid clicks are replaced by organic clicks. These effects do not change significantly before or after the Google-DOJ settlement. In contrast, pharmacies not certified by any of the four major certification agencies – referred to as tier-C sites – suffer the greatest reduction in both paid and organic clicks, and the reduction is exacerbated after the Google-DOJ settlement.

Second, we explore whether the effect of the ban depends on what drug names consumers search for on the Internet. Drug queries that led to more clicks on non-NABP-certified pharmacies before the ban are most affected by the ban, but chronic drug queries are less affected by the ban than non-chronic drugs.

Overall, we conclude that the ban has increased search cost for tier-B sites, but at least some consumers overcome the search cost by switching from paid to organic links. In addition to search cost, our results suggest that the ban may have increased health concerns for tier-C sites and discouraged consumers from reaching them via both paid and organic links. It is also possible that tier-C sites are buried deeper in organic results than tier-A and tier-B sites, and the extra obscurity adds difficulty for consumers to switch to organic links for tier-C sites. Unfortunately, comScore data do not contain the rank information of search results following a specific query. Hence we cannot distinguish the effects of heightened health concerns from organic rank changes after the Google-DOJ settlement.

More generally, our study is limited to consumer search via search engines, as recorded in the comScore data. Due to the lack of individual click-through data, we do not know whether a consumer switches between drug, pharmacy and other queries after the ban of non-NABP-certified pharmacies from sponsored search. Nor do we know whether the banned pharmacies have engineered their organic results or the NABP-certified pharmacies have increased price or changed their advertising strategy after the ban. These supply side questions warrant further study.

References

1. Adams III, A Frank; Robert B. Ekelund Jr. and John D. Jackson (2003): "Occupational Licensing of a Credence Good: The Regulation of Midwifery" Southern Economic Journal, 69(3): 659-675.

2. Bate, Roger; Ginger Zhe Jin and Aparna Mathur (2013): "In Whom We Trust: The Role of Certification Agencies in Online Drug Market", the B.E. Journal of Economics Analysis and Policy. Contribution Tier, Volume 14, Issue 1, Pages 111-150, ISSN (Online) 1935-1682, ISSN (Print) 2194-6108, DOI: 10.1515/bejeap-2013-0085, December 2013.

3. Blake, Thomas; Chris Nosko and Steven Tadelis (2013): "Consumer Heterogeneity and Paid Search Effectiveness: A Large Scale Field Experiment", Working Paper.

4. Chan, David X.; Deepak Kumar, Sheng Ma, and Jim Koehler (2012): "Impact of Ranking Of Organic Search Results On The Incrementality of Search Ads" available at http://static.googleusercontent.com/externalcontent/untrusteddlcp/research.google.com/en/us/pubs/archive/37731.pdf.

5. Chan, David X.; Yuan Yuan, Jim Koehler, and Deepak Kumar (2011): "Incremental Clicks Impact Of Search Advertising", available at http://static.googleusercontent.com/media/research.google.com/en/us/pubs/archive/37161.pdf.

6. Chaudhuri, Shubham; Pinelopi K. Goldberg and Panle Jia (2006): "Estimating the Effects of Global Patent Protection in Pharmaceuticals: A Case Study of Quinolones in India" The American Economic Review 96(5): 1477-1514.

7. Chen, Lu and Joel Waldfogel (2006): "Does Information Undermine Brand? Information Intermediary Use and Preference for Branded Web Retailers." Journal of Industrial Economics, December 2006.

8. Chiou, Lesley and Catherine Tucker (2011): "How Does Pharmaceutical Advertising Affect Consumer Search? (December 1, 2011). Available at SSRN: http://ssrn.com/abstract=1542934 or http://dx.doi.org/10.2139/ssrn.1542934.

9. Dobkin, Carlos and Nancy Nicosia (2009): "TheWar on Drugs: Methamphetamine, Public Health and Crime" American Economic Review 99(1): 324-349.

10. Fox, Susannah (2004): "Prescription drugs online" Washington, DC: Pew Internet & American Life Project; 2004. Oct 10, [2011-08-23]. Available at http://www.pewinternet.org//media/Files/Reports/2004/PIPPrescriptionDrugsOnline.pdf.

11. George, Lisa and Christiaan Hogendorn (2013): "Local News Online: Aggregators, Geo-Targeting and the Market for Local News." CUNY working paper.

12. Gilbert, David; Tom Walley; and Bill New (2000): "Lifestyle Medicines", British Medical Journal, 2000, pp. 321:1341.

13. Gurau C. (2005): "Pharmaceutical marketing on the internet: Marketing techniques and customer profile" Journal of Consumer Marketing 22(7):421.

14. IMS Institute (2011): "The Use of Medicines in the United States: Review of 2010." Accessed at http://www.imshealth.com/deployedfiles/imshealth/Global/Content/IMSInstitute/StaticFile/IHII_UseOfMed_report.pdf on March 20, 2012.

15. Jansen, Bernard J. and Marc Resnick (2006): "An examination of searchers' perceptions of non-sponsored and sponsored links during ecommerce Web searching" Journal of Amer. Soc. Inform. Sci. Technol. 57: 1949–1961.

16. Jansen, Bernard J.; Anna Brown and Marc Resnick (2007): "Factors relating to the decision to click on a sponsored link" Decision Support System: 44, 46-59.

17. Jansen, Bernard J. and Amanda Spink (2009): "Investigating customer click through behaviour with integrated sponsored and nonsponsored results" International Journal of Internet Marketing and Advertising, 5(1/2): 74-94.

18. Law, Marc T. and Sukkoo Kim (2005): "Specialization and Regulation: The Rise of Professionals and the Emergence of Occupational Licensing Regulation" The Journal of Economic History 65(3): 723-756.

19. Law, Marc T. and Mindy S. Marks (2009): "Effects of Occupational Licensing Laws on Minorities: Evidence from the Progressive Era" Journal of Law and Economics, 52(2): 351-366.

20. Leland, Hayne (1979): "Quacks, Lemons and Licensing: A Theory of Minimum Quality Standards" Journal of Political Economy 87:1328–46.

21. NABP (2011): "Internet Drug Outlet Identification Program Progress Report for State and Federal Regulators: January 2011" available at http://www.nabp.net/news/assets/InternetReport1-11.pdf.

22. Orizio, Grazia; Anna Merla; Peter J. Schulz; and Umberto Gelatti (2011): "Quality of Online Pharmacies and Websites Selling Prescription Drugs: A Systematic Review" Journal of Medical Internet Research. 2011 Jul-Sep; 13(3): e74.

23. Pashigian, Peter (1979): "Occupational Licensing and the Interstate Mobility of Professionals" 22(1): 1-25.

24. Peltzman, Sam (1976): "Toward a more general theory of economic regulation" Journal of Law and Economics 19: 211-40.

25. Quon, B.S.; R. Firszt, and M.J. Eisenberg (2005): "A comparison of brand-name drug prices between Canadian-based Internet pharmacies and major U.S. drug chain pharmacies." Annals of Internal Medicine 2005, Sep 20;143(6):397–403.

26. Shapiro, Carl (1986): "Investment, moral hazard, and occupational licensing" Review of Economic Studies 53: 843-62.

27. Shepard, Lawrence (1978): "Licensing Restrictions and the Cost of Dental Care" A Journal of Law and Economics, 21(1): 187-201.

28. Skinner, Brett J. (2005) "Canada's Drug Price Paradox: The Unexpected Losses Caused by Government Interference in Pharmaceutical Markets" The Fraser Institute Digital Publication (February).

29. Skinner, Brett (2006): "Price Controls, Patents, and Cross-Border Internet Pharmacies Risks to Canada's Drug Supply and International Trading Relations" The Fraser Institute, Critical Issues Bulletin 2006. Available at http://www.fraserinstitute.org/research-news/display.aspx?id=13315.

30. Stigler, George J. (1971) "The theory of economic regulation" Bell Journal of Economics and Management Science 1:3-21.

31. Yang, Sha and Anindya Ghose (2010): "Analyzing the Relationship Between Organic and Sponsored Search Advertising: Positive, Negative, or Zero Interdependence?" Marketing Science 29(4): 602–623.

Figures and Tables

Figure 1: Google Search Screenshot, Before the Ban

Figure 2: Google Search Screenshot, After the Ban

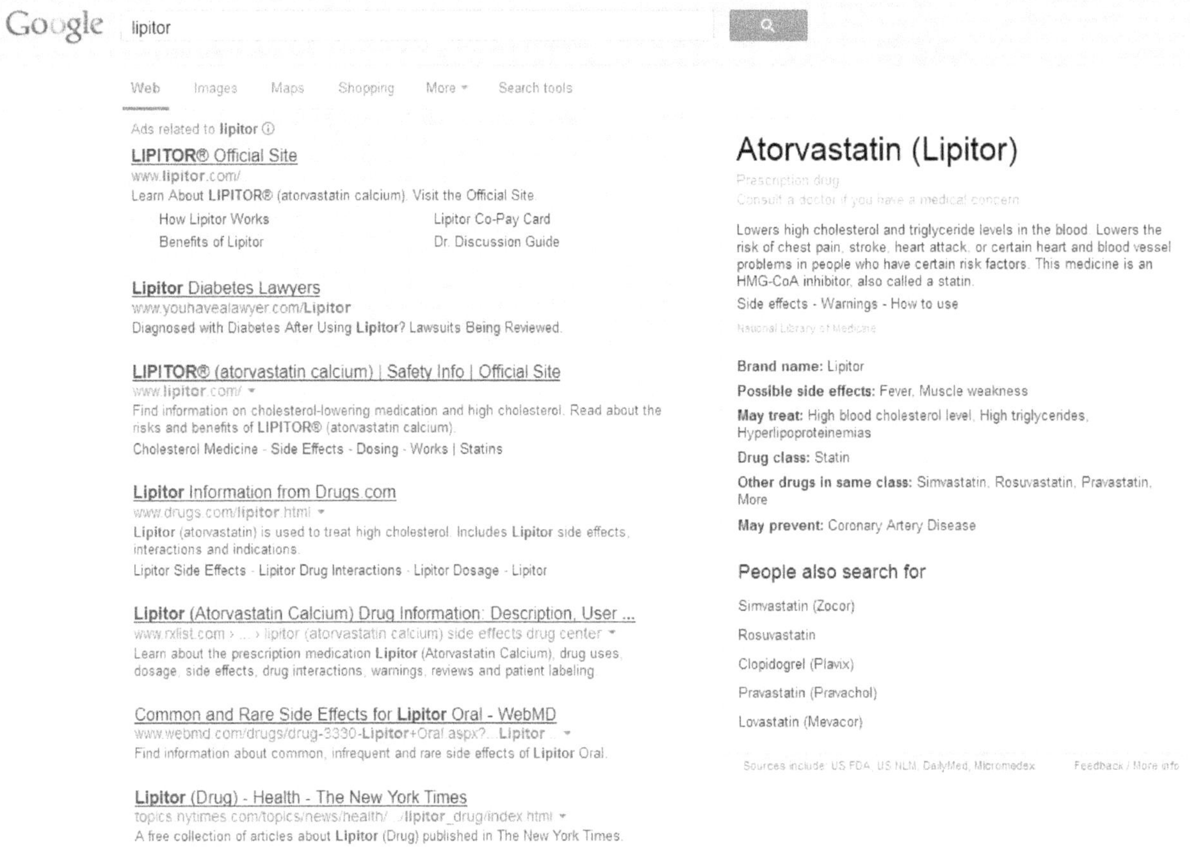

Figure 3: Example ComScore Data

Report:	Term Destinations			
Query:	Lipitor			
Date:	January 2012			
Engine:	All			
Match Option:	Match All Forms			

Key Metrics
Total Clicks	169,156
Paid Clicks	38,670
Organic Clicks	130,486

Site Clicks
Entity Name	lipitor.com	Wal-Mart	walmart.com	...
Entity Level	Property	Property	Media Title	...
SubCategory	778218	778230	778230,778281	...
Organic Clicks	27,228	10,713	10,713	...
Paid Clicks	34,420	2,861	2,861	...

Report:	Term Profile			
Query:	Lipitor			
Date:	January 2012			
Engine:	n/a			
Match Option:	Match All Forms			

Key Metrics
Searches	293,240
Searchers	219,414
Searches per Searcher	1.34

Demographics
Title	HoH Age	Income	Region	...
Level	45-54	$75k-99k	New England	...
Reach	40.15	15.65	2.21	...

Figure 4: Searchers and Searches by Broad Query Type

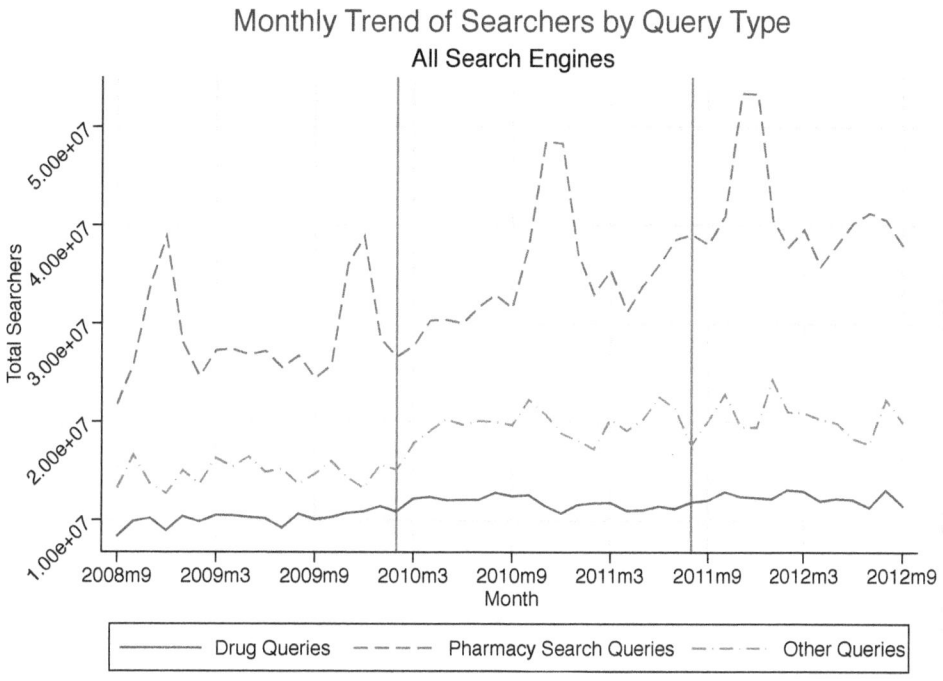

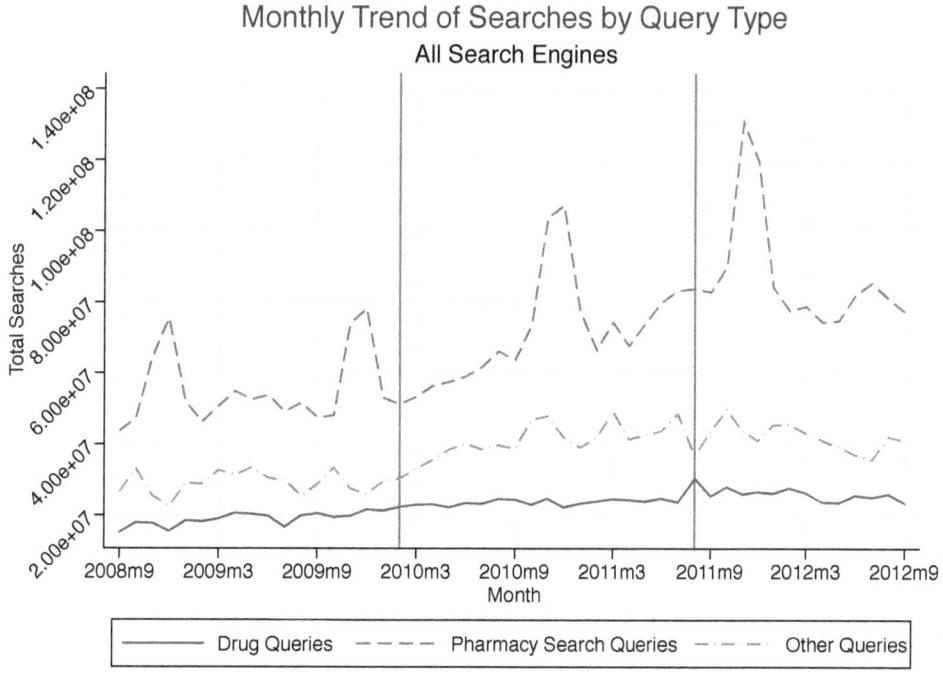

Notes: The top figure plots the total number of searchers of each query type in each month. The bottom figure plots the total number of searches of each query type in each month.

Figure 5: Clicks On Pharmacy Websites

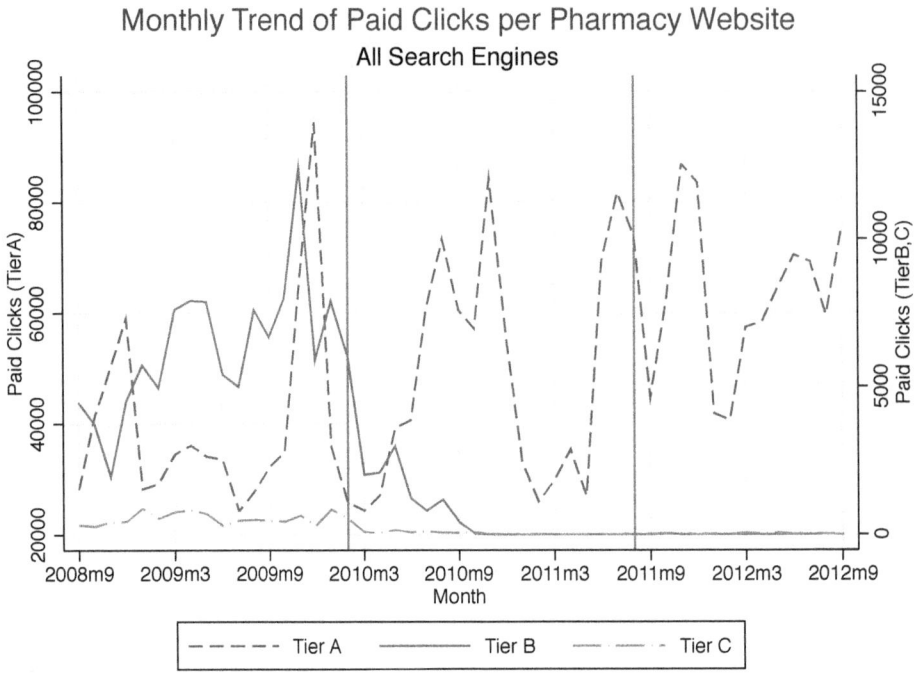

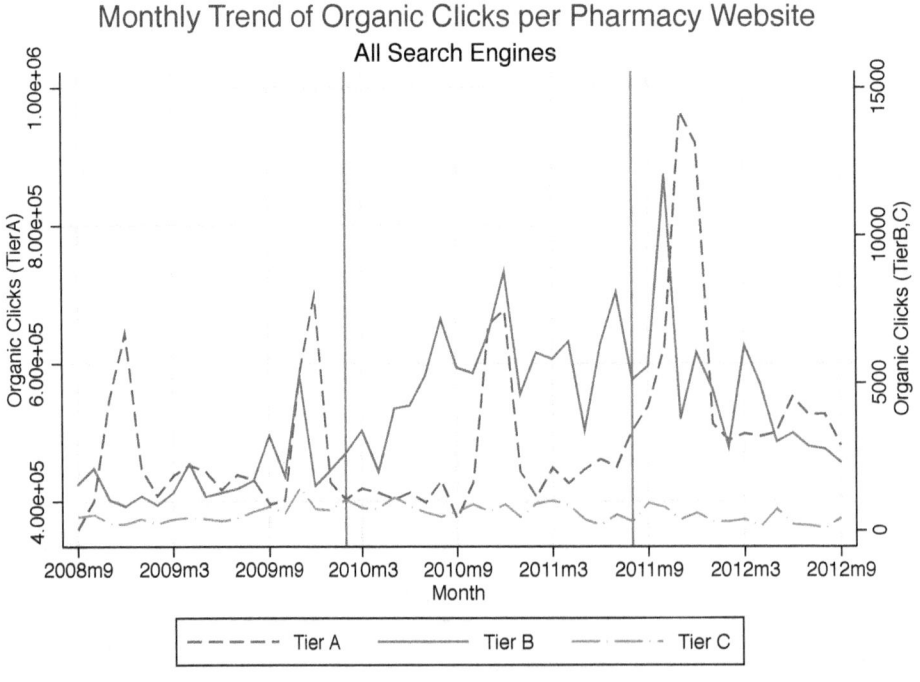

Notes: 1. The figures plot the total monthly paid and organic clicks of each tier of online pharmacy website. The total clicks sum over all types of queries that lead to clicks on online pharmacies. 2. If the ban on sponsored links has been perfectly implemented, we should observe zero paid clicks from Tier-B and Tier-C websites in regime 2. The positive paid clicks on Tier-B websites are on "canadapharmacy.com" in November 2011, and on "northwestpharmacy.com" in August 2012. The positive paid clicks on Tier-C websites are from "freemedicine.com" and "albertsonssavonpharmacies.com".

Figure 6: Pharmacy Searches by Query Type

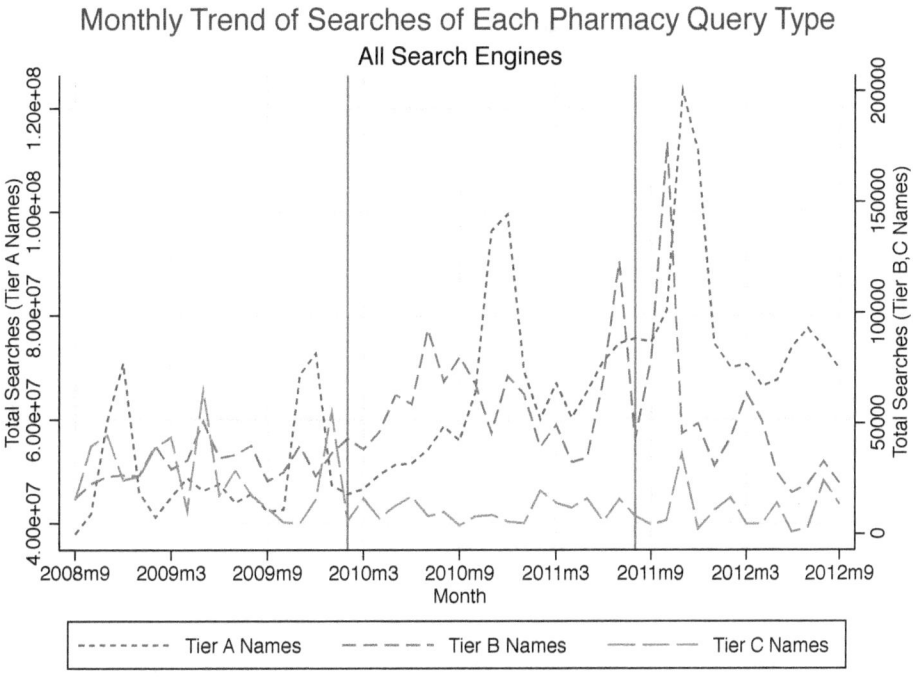

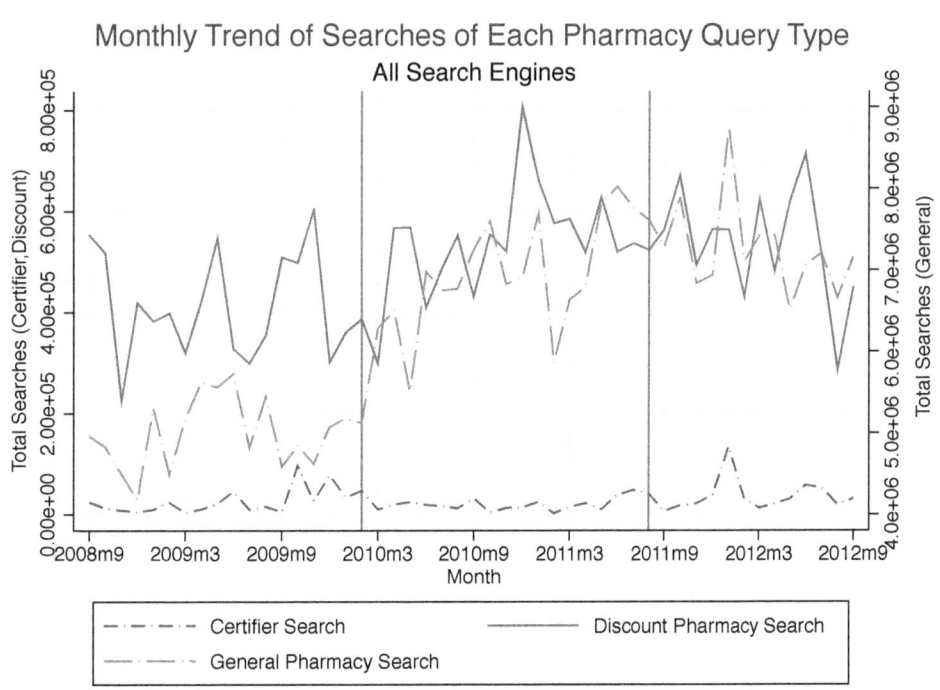

Notes: The top figure plots the total number of searches for each pharmacy tier in each month. The bottom figure plots the total number of searches for other pharmacy-related queries in each month.

Table 1: List of Events

Time	Event
before 2009	Google contracted with PharmacyChecker to filter out uncertified websites
July 2009	Some pharmacies advertising on Google were found to be uncertified by PharmacyChecker
August 2009	LegitScript.com and KnuhOn.com criticized Microsoft for allowing rogue pharmacies to advertise on Bing
November 2009	FDA issued 22 warning letters to website operators
February 9, 2010	Google began to ban non-NABP-certified pharmacies from sponsored ads for US consumers
April 21, 2010	Google contracted with LegitScript to implement the ban
June 10, 2010	Microsoft and Yahoo! started to ban non-NABP-certified pharmacies from sponsored ads for US consumers.
June 22, 2010	Google partnered with the National Institute of Health (NIH) and expanded its search tool to include drug facts with NIH links. This is only available to US consumers.
August 24, 2011	DOJ announced its settlement with Google

Table 2: Regimes

Regime	Time	Policy
Regime 0	September 2008 - January 2010	Google used PharmacyChecker to filter online pharmacy ads
Regime 1	March 2010 - July 2011	Google required NABP-certification and switched to LegitScript in place of PharmacyChecker
Regime 2	September 2011 - September 2012	Google reached an official settlement with DOJ

Notes: February 2010 and August 2011 are excluded because the imposition of the ban and the announcement of the settlement occurred in these two months.

Table 3: Query List

Query Group	Query Type	Count	Examples	Source
Pharmacy	General Pharmacy Keywords	6	pharmacy at	Keywordspy.com
	Discount Pharmacy Keywords	46	cheap drugs	Keywordspy.com
	TierA Pharmacy Names	9	cvs	comScore, cert. websites
	TierB Pharmacy Names	13	jandrugs	comScore, cert. websites
	TierC Pharmacy Names	19	canadamedicineshop	comScore, cert. websites
	Certifier Search	8	vipps	cert. websites
Drug	Prescription Drug Names	263	lipitor	FDA Orange Book, Keywordspy.com
Other	Drug Manufacturer	59	pfizer	Kantar Media
	Information/Gov.	5	fda	comScore
	Information/Info Sites	17	webmd	comScore
	Information/Health Terms	8	panic-anxiety	comScore
	Other Drugs/Non-Online Rx	17	renvela	FDA Orange Book
	Other Drugs/OTC Related	58	prevacid	FDA Orange Book
	Total Count	528		

Table 4: Query Statistics: Overall Number of Searches and Clicks

		Total	PharmClicks/	%Pharmacy	Paid Clicks				Organic Clicks			
Query Type	Reg	Searches*	Search	Clicks	Tier-A	Tier-B	Tier-C		Tier-A	Tier-B	Tier-C	
Pharmacy Queries												
General Pharmacy Search	0	832.6	9.6%	27.9%	94,325	20,843	6,692		306,419	6,312	13,792	
	1	1,156.6	8.3%	39.7%	72,707	2,483	1,390		259,706	16,445	18,972	
	2	1,208.7	6.5%	21.0%	88,117	0	222		268,329	10,373	17,160	
Discount Pharmacy Search	0	9.0	38.9%	66.5%	932	5,889	776		3,673	2,900	3,815	
	1	11.8	33.4%	58.5%	1,825	815	19		3,097	10,353	5,184	
	2	11.7	26.3%	62.4%	1,512	1	0		3,571	10,370	3,166	
Tier-A Pharmacy Names	0	5,546.1	49.8%	80.6%	230,232	71	20		2,883,102	55	183	
	1	7,167.0	51.1%	78.2%	283,555	0	0		2,794,803	105	217	
	2	8,853.2	45.1%	78.8%	380,141	0	0		3,793,243	794	568	
Tier-B Pharmacy Names	0	2.4	50.2%	92.9%	632	366	98		2,088	652	96	
	1	4.7	52.9%	93.0%	721	64	0		1,695	3,319	0	
	2	3.9	50.2%	97.9%	958	0	0		740	3,543	0	
Tier-C Pharmacy Names	0	1.4	47.2%	39.8%	0	0	160		0	0	250	
	1	0.6	47.8%	31.4%	0	0	104		113	0	684	
	2	0.6	0.0%	7.1%	0	0	0		0	0	15	
Certifier Search	0	2.8	117.0%	6.5%	59	0	0		77	0	0	
	1	2.2	0.9%	1.3%	0	0	0		44	0	0	
	2	4.1	3.9%	1.5%	109	0	0		0	0	0	
Drug Queries	0	71.9	14.1%	22.1%	273	1,039	1,092		6,348	63	578	
	1	89.9	2.2%	2.6%	329	238	121		1,750	535	1,439	
	2	97.6	2.6%	3.5%	559	2	111		2,171	713	1,344	

* in thousands

Notes: 1. All statistics in this table are averaging across queries within each query type×month, and the statistics related to clicks are conditional on queries that led to any clicks on any pharmacy website. "Total Searches" is the average monthly searches per query. "PharmClicks/Search" is the average monthly (Pharmacy Website Clicks/Searches) ratio per query. "%Pharmacy Clicks" is the average monthly ratio of clicks on pharmacy websites relative to all clicks following each query. Columns for paid clicks and organic clicks show the number of monthly clicks that land on each tier of pharmacy. 2. The large number of searches on Tier-A pharmacy names is due to the discount chains that also sell general products besides drugs. 3. The pharmacy clicks to search ratio for Tier-C queries in regime 2 is not precisely zero, but we cannot calculate the ratio due to censoring.

Table 5: Pharmacy Website Statistics

		Mean		Median		StdDev		25 percentile		75 percentile		$\underline{N}$	$\underline{N}$	$\underline{N}$
	Regime	paid	organic	paid	organic	paid	organic	paid	organic	paid	organic	active	(Paid>0)	(Organic>0)
TierA	0	40,538	466,980	0	627	138,298	2,078,990	0	0	412	7,566	47	23	36
	1	48,571	452,544	0	680	206,487	2,075,955	0	0	132	8,071	50	19	39
	2	62,696	586,653	0	567	228,356	2,820,957	0	0	175	5,119	48	19	34
TierB	0	6,338	1,795	735	217	10,168	3,640	0	0	7,929	2,058	26	17	17
	1	633	5,476	0	824	1,105	10,870	0	108	1,137	3,712	27	13	24
	2	2	4,652	0	1,078	8	7,376	0	0	0	5,201	25	2	17
TierC	0	544	522	0	0	2,593	1,495	0	0	0	189	138	28	74
	1	39	694	0	0	244	2,932	0	0	0	56	132	14	59
	2	18	417	0	0	223	1,787	0	0	0	0	92	2	40

Notes: 1. The click counts in the table are at the month×website level and the statistics are calculated for each website type×regime. We keep the balanced sample of websites, (57 tier-A websites, 28 tier-B websites, and 181 tier-C websites) in calculating the statistics. 2. We define active websites as websites having received either censored or positive clicks from the set of queries in our data. The last three columns report the number of websites in each regime that are active, have positive (non-censored) paid clicks, and have positive (non-censored) organic clicks.

Table 6: Regression Results: Clicks on Online Pharmacy Websites (from All Queries)

	(1)	(2)	(3)	(4)	(5)
	I(AnyClicks)	I(TtlClicks>0)	Ln(TtlClicks)	I(OrgClicks>0)	Ln(OrgClicks)
TierB	0.128	0.0990		-0.0780	
	(0.231)	(0.253)		(0.250)	
TierC	-0.534***	-0.788***		-0.895***	
	(0.159)	(0.170)		(0.168)	
Regime1	0.0520	0.0158	0.176	0.0158	0.199*
	(0.0484)	(0.0450)	(0.104)	(0.0449)	(0.108)
TierB×Regime1	0.0960	-0.144	-0.617**	0.0114	0.882***
	(0.160)	(0.134)	(0.253)	(0.122)	(0.245)
TierC×Regime1	-0.230***	-0.260***	-0.140	-0.172**	0.130
	(0.0769)	(0.0897)	(0.198)	(0.0843)	(0.186)
Regime2	-0.0231	-0.0871	0.151	-0.0924	0.146
	(0.0747)	(0.0692)	(0.130)	(0.0685)	(0.121)
TierB×Regime2	0.0668	-0.0384	-0.583**	0.149	1.136***
	(0.171)	(0.146)	(0.255)	(0.134)	(0.255)
TierC×Regime2	-0.480***	-0.424***	-0.0197	-0.323***	0.247
	(0.111)	(0.127)	(0.230)	(0.119)	(0.222)
Constant	0.0790	-0.189	9.043***	-0.194	8.508***
	(0.141)	(0.146)	(0.0489)	(0.146)	(0.0484)
Marginal Effect					
TierB×Regime1	0.0328	-0.037		0.0028	
	(0.0546)	(0.0345)		(0.0302)	
TierC×Regime1	-0.0785***	-0.0669***		-0.0426**	
	(0.0251)	(0.0228)		(0.0206)	
TierB×Regime2	0.0228	-0.0099		0.037	
	(0.0583)	(0.0376)		(0.0332)	
TierC×Regime2	-0.164***	-0.1092***		-0.08***	
	(0.0378)	(0.0329)		(0.0297)	
Observations	12,502	12,502	2,698	12,502	2,552
FE	-	-	Website	-	Website

Notes: Standard errors in parentheses. * $p < 0.10$, ** $p < 0.05$, *** $p < 0.01$.
1. Dummy variables for Tier-A pharmacies, regime 0, and their interactions are excluded from the regression. 2. This table examines the differential changes in total and organic clicks outcome in each regime. Dependent variable in column (1) is if a website had any clicks, paid or organic, *including censored clicks*, in a given month. Dependent variables in columns (2) and (4) are if a website has any *non-censored* positive total or organic clicks in a given month, respectively. Dependent variables in columns (3) and (5) are the number of non-censored positive total and organic clicks (respectively) on a website when the number of clicks is non-censored and positive. 3. Standard errors are clustered at the website level for all regressions. 4. In counting the total number of clicks into each website, we included clicks from all types of queries - pharmacy queries, drug queries and other queries.

Table 7: Regression Results: Searchers and Searches of Pharmacy Queries

	Ln(Searchers)	Ln(Searches)
Regime1×TierBQuery	-0.258	-0.260
	(0.585)	(0.598)
Regime1×TierCQuery	-1.487*	-1.550*
	(0.616)	(0.628)
Regime1×Certifier	-0.415	-0.426
	(0.482)	(0.485)
Regime1×General	-0.329	-0.252
	(0.555)	(0.573)
Regime1×Discount	-0.188	-0.151
	(0.498)	(0.504)
Regime1	0.612	0.624
	(0.468)	(0.472)
Regime2×TierBQuery	-0.687	-0.749
	(0.722)	(0.729)
Regime2×TierCQuery	-1.916**	-2.085**
	(0.659)	(0.663)
Regime2×Certifier	0.367	0.333
	(0.731)	(0.755)
Regime2×General	0.129	0.0982
	(0.687)	(0.699)
Regime2×Discount	-0.242	-0.281
	(0.619)	(0.623)
Regime2	0.418	0.475
	(0.583)	(0.585)
Constant	4.273***	4.456***
	(0.0758)	(0.0781)
Observations	4,794	4,794
Fixed Effects	Query	Query

Standard errors in parentheses. * $p<0.10$, ** $p<0.05$, *** $p<0.01$.
Notes: 1. Tier-A pharmacy names and regime 0 are excluded. 2. An observation is at the query×month level, and outcome variable is the log level of the total searchers and searches for a query in a month. 3. Standard errors are clustered at the query level.

Table 8: Regression Results: Total Clicks on Online Pharmacy Websites (from Pharmacy Queries)

Covariates	$I(TotalClicks>0)$			$Ln(TotalClicks)$		
	1×	TierB ×	TierC ×	1×	TierB ×	TierC ×
Marginal Effect						
Regime1	0.0078	-0.0498***	-0.0215**	0.305	-0.108	-0.230
	(0.0063)	(0.0254)	(0.0146)	(0.170)	(0.311)	(0.395)
Regime2	-0.0017	-0.0451**	-0.0238	0.466**	1.925*	0.799*
	(0.0069)	(0.029)	(0.0181)	(0.147)	(0.761)	(0.323)
TierB Query	-0.112***	0.2005***	0.0709**	-6.382***	7.578***	6.809***
	(0.0085)	(0.0177)	(0.0168)	(0.779)	(0.842)	(0.923)
TierC Query	-0.5412***		0.5608***	-6.981***		7.741***
	(0.0135)		(0.0063)	(0.776)		(0.679)
Discount	-0.0644***	0.2385***	0.1635***	-4.294***	6.898***	5.832***
	(0.0072)	(0.0165)	(0.0123)	(0.998)	(1.078)	(1.039)
General	0.0375***	0.14***	0.0864***	-1.228	2.585**	1.639*
	(0.0062)	(0.0161)	(0.0116)	(0.725)	(0.775)	(0.783)
TierBQuery×Regime1	-0.0289***	0.0675***		-0.312	0.942	
	(0.0124)	(0.0296)		(0.238)	(0.507)	
TierCQuery×Regime1	0.2878***		-0.2946***	0.475		
	(0.0329)		(0.0338)	(0.626)		
Discount×Regime1	-0.0136**	0.0315	0.0143	-0.000350	0.155	0.0803
	(0.0103)	(0.028)	(0.0178)	(0.243)	(0.442)	(0.471)
General×Regime1	-0.0081	0.0187	0.0029	-0.181	-0.0185	0.484
	(0.0087)	(0.0275)	(0.0167)	(0.184)	(0.380)	(0.422)
TierBQuery×Regime2	-0.0539***	0.0814***		0.123	-1.254	
	(0.0165)	(0.0349)		(0.332)	(0.721)	
TierCQuery×Regime2	0.002***		-0.0689**			-2.351***
	(0)		(0.0339)			(0.341)
Discount×Regime2	-0.0229**	0.057**	0.0108	0.303	-2.456**	-1.434**
	(0.0116)	(0.0318)	(0.0216)	(0.387)	(0.766)	(0.496)
General×Regime2	-0.0071	0.003	-0.0291	-0.504**	-1.944**	0.104
	(0.0095)	(0.0312)	(0.0204)	(0.170)	(0.656)	(0.435)
Constant		-0.1471***	-0.1947***	8.424***		
		(0.013)	(0.0102)	(0.275)		
Observations	51,465			6,700		
FE	-			Website		

Standard errors in parentheses. * $p<0.10$, ** $p<0.05$, *** $p<0.01$.

Notes: 1. We used a subsample of clicks on pharmacy websites following pharmacy-related queries. Dummy variables for query type "TierA Names", TierA pharmacies, regime 0, and their interactions are excluded in the regression. 2. The regressions examine the differential changes in the total clicks in each regime from different types of pharmacy queries. In the extensive margin specification, the dependent variable is whether a website recorded any non-censored clicks from one type of pharmacy query in a given month. In the intensive margin specification, the dependent variable is the number of clicks on a website from one type of pharmacy query at a given month, conditional on positive clicks. 3. Coefficients for the extensive margin regression are in the first three columns and the intensive margin regression are in the last three columns. The coefficients for the cross product with a TierB destination website are in columns (2) and (5) and the cross product with a TierC destination website are in columns (4) and (6). 4. Some coefficient estimates were not identified due to too few observations (e.g., comScore recorded no clicks on TierB pharmacies following a query for a TierC pharmacy name). 5. Standard errors are clustered at the website level for all regressions.

Table 9: Regression Results: Online Pharmacy Clicks from H-Drug Vs. L-Drug Queries

	(1)	(2)	(3)	(4)
	$I(Ttlclicks>0)$	$Ln(TtlClicks)$	$I(OrgClicks>0)$	$Ln(OrgClicks)$
Regime1	0.0095	-0.990	0.0046	-1.336**
	(0.0077)	(0.617)	(0.0083)	(0.591)
Regime2	-0.0088	-0.990***	-0.0071	-0.908
	(0.0108)	(0.566)	(0.009)	(0.748)
H-Drug	0.0593***	0.0287	0.0437***	-0.00259
	(0.0194)	(0.397)	(0.0166)	(0.318)
H-Drug×Regime1	-0.0223***	1.204**	-0.009	1.091
	(0.0095)	(0.524)	(0.0081)	(0.690)
H-Drug×Regime2	0.0025	1.623*	0.0121	1.017*
	(0.0167)	(0.301)	(0.0152)	(0.312)
TierB	-0.0104		-0.0957*	
	(0.0355)		(0.049)	
TierB×Regime1	-0.0526**	1.324	0.044	0.173
	(0.0249)	(0.895)	(0.0361)	(0.691)
TierB×Regime2	-0.0634***	1.716	0.0392	-0.0910
	(0.0263)	(1.095)	(0.0306)	(1.073)
H-Drug×TierB	0.0918***	1.464***	0.1206***	-1.622*
	(0.0304)	(0.819)	(0.0425)	(0.389)
H-Drug×TierB×Regime1	-0.0207	-2.425**	-0.0624	0.734
	(0.0247)	(1.029)	(0.0388)	(0.817)
H-Drug×TierB×Regime2	-0.0377	-3.554*	-0.0745**	0.620
	(0.0272)	(1.088)	(0.0358)	(0.842)
TierC	-0.0806**		-0.0797**	
	(0.039)		(0.039)	
TierC×Regime1	-0.0348*	2.330*	-0.009	2.845*
	(0.0182)	(0.859)	(0.0173)	(0.791)
TierC×Regime2	-0.0563*	2.598*	-0.0412	3.137*
	(0.0308)	(0.878)	(0.0311)	(0.936)
H-Drug×TierC	0.0776***	0.708	0.0816***	0.630
	(0.0293)	(0.566)	(0.0296)	(0.531)
H-Drug×TierC×Regime1	0.0006	-2.727*	-0.0189	-2.517*
	(0.0203)	(0.819)	(0.0196)	(0.901)
H-Drug×TierC×Regime2	-0.0145	-3.452*	-0.0213	-3.320*
	(0.0323)	(0.799)	(0.0341)	(0.722)
Constant		7.668*		7.747*
		(0.269)		(0.245)
Observations	14,060	921	14,060	754
FE	-	Website	-	Website

Standard errors in parentheses. * $p < 0.10$, ** $p < 0.05$, *** $p < 0.01$.

Notes: 1. Dummy variables for Tier-A pharmacies, regime 0, and their interactions are excluded from the regression. 2. This table examines the heterogeneous changes in total and organic clicks in each regime resulting from H-Drug and L-Drug queries. The dependent variables in columns (1) and (3) are indicators if a website had any non-censored total or organic clicks in a given month, and the columns report the marginal effects of a probit regression. The dependent variables in columns (2) and (4) are the number of non-censored total and organic clicks on a website when the number of clicks is non-censored and positive. 3. H-Drug and L-Drug are defined by their ratio of clicks into Tier-B and Tier-C websites in the first nine months of the sample (2008/09 - 2009/05). 4. We exclude the first 9 months of observations from the sample as clicks during that time were used to define H and L drugs queries. 5. Some coefficient estimates were not identified due to too few observations. 6. Standard errors are clustered at the website level for all regressions.

Table 10: Regression Results: Online Pharmacies Clicks from Lifestyle Vs. Non-lifestyle Drug Queries

	(1) I(Ttlclicks>0)	(2) Ln(TtlClicks)	(3) I(OrgClicks>0)	(4) Ln(OrgClicks)
Regime1	-0.0032	-0.207	0.0065	-0.713
	(0.0176)	(0.526)	(0.0128)	(0.555)
Regime2	-0.0173	0.00661	0.001	-0.515
	(0.0208)	(0.574)	(0.0163)	(0.596)
Lifestyle (LS)	-0.0359*	-0.308***	-0.0109	-0.320
	(0.019)	(0.171)	(0.0082)	(0.256)
LS×Regime1	0.0257*	0.116	0.0066	0.174
	(0.0151)	(0.241)	(0.0065)	(0.319)
LS×Regime2	0.0537***	0.290	0.0231	0.376
	(0.0211)	(0.270)	(0.0158)	(0.253)
TierB	0.0955***		0.0149	
	(0.038)		(0.03)	
TierB×Regime1	-0.114***	-0.0200	-0.0278	1.863*
	(0.0317)	(0.621)	(0.0218)	(0.693)
TierB×Regime2	-0.116***	-0.403	-0.0234	1.765**
	(0.0394)	(0.651)	(0.0289)	(0.791)
LS×TierB	0.0041	0.557	0.0138	0.583
	(0.0324)	(0.366)	(0.0285)	(0.369)
LS×TierB×Regime1	0.0172	-0.681	0.0026	-0.646
	(0.0305)	(0.541)	(0.0193)	(0.708)
LS×TierB×Regime2	-0.019	-0.860***	-0.0236	-0.704
	(0.0442)	(0.484)	(0.031)	(0.526)
TierC	-0.0436		-0.0332	
	(0.0346)		(0.0293)	
TierC×Regime1	-0.0657***	0.713	-0.0439**	1.291**
	(0.0264)	(0.568)	(0.0197)	(0.584)
TierC×Regime2	-0.0588	0.474	-0.0512*	0.900
	(0.0362)	(0.644)	(0.0278)	(0.667)
LS×TierC	0.0733***	0.760*	0.0392*	0.613***
	(0.0274)	(0.283)	(0.02)	(0.349)
LS×TierC×Regime1	0.0035	-0.626	0.0171	-0.366
	(0.0248)	(0.470)	(0.0189)	(0.490)
LS×TierC×Regime2	-0.0656*	-0.708	-0.0257	-0.437
	(0.0354)	(0.592)	(0.0288)	(0.633)
Constant		7.901*		7.390*
		(0.141)		(0.179)
Observations	18330	1439	18330	1064
FE	-	Website	-	Website

Standard errors in parentheses. * $p < 0.10$, ** $p < 0.05$, *** $p < 0.01$.

Notes: 1. Dummy variables for Tier-A pharmacies, regime 0, and their interactions are excluded from the regression. 2. This table examines the heterogeneous changes in total and organic clicks in each regime led by lifestyle and non-lifestyle drug queries. The dependent variables in columns (1) and (3) are if a website has any non-censored positive total or paid clicks in a given month, and the columns report the marginal effects of the probit regression. The dependent variables in columns (2) and (4) are the number of non-censored positive total and paid clicks on a website when the number of clicks is non-censored and positive. 3. Some coefficient estimates were not identified due to too few observations. 4. Standard errors are clustered at the website level for all regressions.

Table 11: Regression Results: Online Pharmacy Clicks from Chronic Vs. Non-chronic Drugs Queries

	(1) I(Ttlclicks>0)	(2) Ln(TtlClicks)	(3) I(OrgClicks>0)	(4) Ln(OrgClicks)
Regime1	0.0142	-0.137	0.0178	-0.730
	(0.0205)	(0.746)	(0.0174)	(0.802)
Regime2	0.0259	0.178	0.0303	-0.544
	(0.0254)	(0.914)	(0.0195)	(0.901)
Chronic	-0.0183	0.264	-0.0156	0.0257
	(0.0156)	(0.191)	(0.0101)	(0.370)
Chronic×Regime1	-0.0025	-0.857**	-0.0102	-0.553
	(0.0094)	(0.393)	(0.008)	(0.629)
Chronic×Regime2	-0.0187	-0.742*	-0.0169	-0.274
	(0.0197)	(0.278)	(0.0128)	(0.202)
TierB	0.0936***		0.0292	
	(0.0376)		(0.0333)	
TierB×Regime1	-0.1021***	-0.536	-0.0372	1.337
	(0.0306)	(0.801)	(0.0235)	(0.896)
TierB×Regime2	-0.1339***	-1.079	-0.0563**	1.380
	(0.0377)	(0.953)	(0.0258)	(0.948)
Chronic×TierB	-0.0118	-0.640	-0.0221	-0.409
	(0.0276)	(0.428)	(0.027)	(0.479)
Chronic×TierB×Regime1	-0.038	1.558**	0.0006	1.228
	(0.0233)	(0.758)	(0.0199)	(0.900)
Chronic×TierB×Regime2	0.0134	1.373*	0.026	1.009***
	(0.0364)	(0.516)	(0.0278)	(0.520)
TierC	0.0143		0.0092	
	(0.032)		(0.0276)	
TierC×Regime1	-0.0628***	0.452	-0.0415**	1.209
	(0.0265)	(0.801)	(0.0209)	(0.850)
TierC×Regime2	-0.1053***	0.181	-0.0789***	1.052
	(0.0327)	(0.948)	(0.0245)	(0.939)
Chronic×TierC	-0.0567***	-0.695*	-0.057***	-0.323
	(0.0239)	(0.239)	(0.0212)	(0.419)
Chronic×TierC×Regime1	-0.0012	1.325**	0.0196	0.791
	(0.021)	(0.521)	(0.0176)	(0.730)
Chronic×TierC×Regime2	0.0295	1.877*	0.0283	1.158***
	(0.0367)	(0.438)	(0.0265)	(0.596)
Constant		8.035*		7.639*
		(0.141)		(0.154)
Observations	16920	1171	16920	853
FE	-	Website	-	Website

Standard errors in parentheses. * $p < 0.10$, ** $p < 0.05$, *** $p < 0.01$.
Notes: 1. Dummy variables for Tier-A pharmacies, regime 0, and their interactions are excluded from the regression. 2. This table examines the heterogeneous changes in total and organic clicks in each regime led by chronic and non-chronic drug queries. The dependent variables in columns (1) and (3) are if a website has any non-censored positive total or paid clicks in a given month, and the columns report the marginal effects of the probit regression. The dependent variables in columns (2) and (4) are the number of non-censored positive total and paid clicks on a website when the number of clicks is non-censored and positive. 3. Some coefficient estimates were not identified due to too few observations. 4. Standard errors are clustered at the website level for all regressions.

Appendix

Table A1: Examples of H-Drugs and L-Drugs

Top 10 H-Drugs by Total Clicks

Rank	Query	Total Clicks^a	Tier-BC Ratio^b	May Treat
1	viagra	2,890,258	88%	ED*
2	phentermine	2,140,199	52%	over weight, controlled substance
3	xanax	1,866,525	21%	depression, insomnia, controlled substance
4	cialis	1,056,012	87%	ED*
5	oxycodone	829,212	5%	pain, controlled substance
6	insulin	744,736	15%	diabetes
7	ambien	697,907	6%	sleep aid, controlled substance
8	effexor	656,777	6%	depression
9	cymbalta	648,823	10%	depression
10	oxycontin	553,726	16%	pain, controlled substance

Top 10 L-Drugs by Total Clicks

Rank	Query	Total Clicks^a	Tier-BC Ratio^b	May Treat
1	coumadin	729,570	0%	blood clots
2	metoprolol	516,298	0%	high blood pressure
3	flexeril	409,765	0%	pain
4	keflex	307,195	0%	bacterial infections
5	skelaxin	243,452	0%	pain
6	bystolic	224,755	0%	high blood pressure
7	omnicef	184,677	0%	infections
8	strattera	138,808	0%	attention-deficit/hyperactivity disorder
9	zyprexa	133,542	0%	psychotic mental disorders
10	lupron	132,092	0%	advanced prostate cancer

* ED stands for erectile dysfunction.

Notes: ^{a} Total Clicks is the total number of clicks on online pharmacy websites following each search query from September 2008 to September 2011. The drugs in each category are ranked by this total number of clicks. ^{b} Tier-B,C ratio is the percentage of total clicks from each query that led to Tier-B and Tier-C sites in the first nine months of the sample (2008/09 - 2009/05). A drug query is defined as an H-Drug is the Tier-B,C ratio is greater than 3%, and is defined as L-Drug when the Tier-B,C ratio is smaller than 0.1%. In total, we have 79 H-Drug queries and 112 L-Drug queries.

Table 11: Regression Results: Online Pharmacy Clicks from Chronic Vs. Non-chronic Drugs Queries

	(1) $I(Ttlclicks>0)$	(2) $Ln(TtlClicks)$	(3) $I(OrgClicks>0)$	(4) $Ln(OrgClicks)$
Regime1	0.0142	-0.137	0.0178	-0.730
	(0.0205)	(0.746)	(0.0174)	(0.802)
Regime2	0.0259	0.178	0.0303	-0.544
	(0.0254)	(0.914)	(0.0195)	(0.901)
Chronic	-0.0183	0.264	-0.0156	0.0257
	(0.0156)	(0.191)	(0.0101)	(0.370)
Chronic×Regime1	-0.0025	-0.857**	-0.0102	-0.553
	(0.0094)	(0.393)	(0.008)	(0.629)
Chronic×Regime2	-0.0187	-0.742*	-0.0169	-0.274
	(0.0197)	(0.278)	(0.0128)	(0.202)
TierB	0.0936***		0.0292	
	(0.0376)		(0.0333)	
TierB×Regime1	-0.1021***	-0.536	-0.0372	1.337
	(0.0306)	(0.801)	(0.0235)	(0.896)
TierB×Regime2	-0.1339***	-1.079	-0.0563**	1.380
	(0.0377)	(0.953)	(0.0258)	(0.948)
Chronic×TierB	-0.0118	-0.640	-0.0221	-0.409
	(0.0276)	(0.428)	(0.027)	(0.479)
Chronic×TierB×Regime1	-0.038	1.558**	0.0006	1.228
	(0.0233)	(0.758)	(0.0199)	(0.900)
Chronic×TierB×Regime2	0.0134	1.373*	0.026	1.009***
	(0.0364)	(0.516)	(0.0278)	(0.520)
TierC	0.0143		0.0092	
	(0.032)		(0.0276)	
TierC×Regime1	-0.0628***	0.452	-0.0415**	1.209
	(0.0265)	(0.801)	(0.0209)	(0.850)
TierC×Regime2	-0.1053***	0.181	-0.0789***	1.052
	(0.0327)	(0.948)	(0.0245)	(0.939)
Chronic×TierC	-0.0567***	-0.695*	-0.057***	-0.323
	(0.0239)	(0.239)	(0.0212)	(0.419)
Chronic×TierC×Regime1	-0.0012	1.325**	0.0196	0.791
	(0.021)	(0.521)	(0.0176)	(0.730)
Chronic×TierC×Regime2	0.0295	1.877*	0.0283	1.158***
	(0.0367)	(0.438)	(0.0265)	(0.596)
Constant		8.035*		7.639*
		(0.141)		(0.154)
Observations	16920	1171	16920	853
FE	-	Website	-	Website

Standard errors in parentheses. * $p < 0.10$, ** $p < 0.05$, *** $p < 0.01$.
Notes: 1. Dummy variables for Tier-A pharmacies, regime 0, and their interactions are excluded from the regression. 2. This table examines the heterogeneous changes in total and organic clicks in each regime led by chronic and non-chronic drug queries. The dependent variables in columns (1) and (3) are if a website has any non-censored positive total or paid clicks in a given month, and the columns report the marginal effects of the probit regression. The dependent variables in columns (2) and (4) are the number of non-censored positive total and paid clicks on a website when the number of clicks is non-censored and positive. 3. Some coefficient estimates were not identified due to too few observations. 4. Standard errors are clustered at the website level for all regressions.

Appendix

Table A1: Examples of H-Drugs and L-Drugs

Top 10 H-Drugs by Total Clicks

Rank	Query	Total Clicks[a]	Tier-BC Ratio[b]	May Treat
1	viagra	2,890,258	88%	ED*
2	phentermine	2,140,199	52%	over weight, controlled substance
3	xanax	1,866,525	21%	depression, insomnia, controlled substance
4	cialis	1,056,012	87%	ED*
5	oxycodone	829,212	5%	pain, controlled substance
6	insulin	744,736	15%	diabetes
7	ambien	697,907	6%	sleep aid, controlled substance
8	effexor	656,777	6%	depression
9	cymbalta	648,823	10%	depression
10	oxycontin	553,726	16%	pain, controlled substance

Top 10 L-Drugs by Total Clicks

Rank	Query	Total Clicks[a]	Tier-BC Ratio[b]	May Treat
1	coumadin	729,570	0%	blood clots
2	metoprolol	516,298	0%	high blood pressure
3	flexeril	409,765	0%	pain
4	keflex	307,195	0%	bacterial infections
5	skelaxin	243,452	0%	pain
6	bystolic	224,755	0%	high blood pressure
7	omnicef	184,677	0%	infections
8	strattera	138,808	0%	attention-deficit/hyperactivity disorder
9	zyprexa	133,542	0%	psychotic mental disorders
10	lupron	132,092	0%	advanced prostate cancer

* ED stands for erectile dysfunction.

Notes: [a] Total Clicks is the total number of clicks on online pharmacy websites following each search query from September 2008 to September 2011. The drugs in each category are ranked by this total number of clicks. [b] Tier-B,C ratio is the percentage of total clicks from each query that led to Tier-B and Tier-C sites in the first nine months of the sample (2008/09 - 2009/05). A drug query is defined as an H-Drug is the Tier-B,C ratio is greater than 3%, and is defined as L-Drug when the Tier-B,C ratio is smaller than 0.1%. In total, we have 79 H-Drug queries and 112 L-Drug queries.

Table A2: Examples of Lifestyle and Non-Lifestyle Drugs

Top 10 Lifestyle Drugs

Rank	Query	Total Clicks[a]	Tier-BC Ratio[b]	May Treat
1	viagra	2,890,258	36.6%	ED*
2	phentermine	2,140,199	51.7%	over weight, controlled substance
3	xanax	1,866,525	20.3%	depression, insomnia, controlled substance
4	cialis	1,056,012	23.3%	ED*
5	oxycodone	829,212	5.1%	pain, controlled substance
6	ambien	697,907	6.4%	sleep aid, controlled substance
7	oxycontin	553,726	15.9%	pain, controlled substance
8	botox	420,769	0.7%	wrinkle, face lift
9	levitra	367,965	13.9%	ED*
10	soma	327,303	6.9%	pain and stiffness of muscle spasms

Top 10 Non-Lifestyle Drugs

Rank	Query	Total Clicks[a]	Tier-BC Ratio[b]	May Treat
1	lexapro	1,053,639	0.0%	depression
2	zoloft	817,323	0.1%	depression
3	suboxone	811,330	1.6%	chronic pain
4	insulin	744,736	1.0%	diabetes
5	coumadin	729,570	0.0%	blood clots
6	effexor	656,777	0.5%	depression
7	cymbalta	648,823	0.3%	depression
8	prozac	639,980	1.5%	depression
9	synthroid	529,037	0.4%	hypothyroidism
10	metoprolol	516,298	0.0%	high blood pressure

* ED stands for erectile dysfunction.

Notes: [a] Total Clicks is the total number of clicks on online pharmacy websites following each search query from September 2008 to September 2011. The drugs in each category are ranked by the total number of clicks. [b] Tier-BC Ratio is the percentage of total clicks from the query that landed on TierB and TierC sites in the first nine months of the sample.

Table A3: Examples of Chronic and Non-Chronic Drugs

Top 10 Chronic Drugs

Rank	Query	Total Clicks[a]	Tier-BC Ratio[b]	Prescription Freq.[c]	May Treat
1	lexapro	1,053,639	0.0%	5.5	depression
2	zoloft	817,323	0.1%	5.1	depression
3	effexor	656,777	0.5%	5.3	depression
4	cymbalta	648,823	0.3%	6.3	depression
5	oxycontin	553,726	15.9%	5.1	pain, controlled substance
6	synthroid	529,037	0.4%	5.7	hypothyroidism
7	metoprolol	516,298	0.0%	5.7	high blood pressure
8	gabapentin	507,686	1.0%	5.6	seizures
9	pristiq	440,084	2.3%	5.0	depression
10	seroquel	438846	0.8%	6.2	schizophrenia

Top 10 Non-Chronic Drugs

Rank	Query	Total Clicks[a]	Tier-BC Ratio[b]	Prescription Freq.[c]	May Treat
1	viagra	2,890,258	36.6%	3.2	ED*
2	xanax	1,866,525	20.3%	2.5	depression, insomnia, controlled substance
3	cialis	1,056,012	23.3%	2.6	ED*
4	oxycodone	829,212	5.1%	3.4	pain, controlled substance
5	celexa	459,163	0.2%	1.0	depression
6	flexeril	409,765	0%	2.2	pain and stiffness of muscle spasms
7	levitra	367,965	13.9%	3.2	ED*
8	metronidazole	340,345	14.5%	1.9	bacterial infections
9	keflex	307,195	0%	1.5	bacterial infections
10	zithromax	295,800	45.6%	1.2	bacterial infections

* ED stands for erectile dysfunction.

Notes: [a] Total Clicks is the total number of clicks on online pharmacy websites following the search query from September 2008 to September 2011. The drugs in each category are ranked by the total number of clicks. [b] Tier-B,C ratio is the percentage of total clicks from each query that led to Tier-B and Tier-C sites in the first nine months of the sample (2008/09 - 2009/05). [c] Prescriptions Freq.(frequency) is the average number of prescriptions for each patient in a given year. It is calculated from 2010 Medical Expenditure Panel Survey and is weighted to reflect the national representative statistics. When the average number of prescriptions is higher than 5, we define the drug as chronic, while if it is below 3.5, we define the drug as non-chronic.

www.ingramcontent.com/pod-product-compliance
Lightning Source LLC
Chambersburg PA
CBHW081910170526
45167CB00007B/3229